SMALL-TOWN
WISCONSIN

Fun, Surprising, and Exceptional Road Trips

MARY BERGIN

Globe
Pequot

Essex, Connecticut

For my lifelong friend Marjean and long-ago Oshkosh housemates—the girls of 812—who understand and appreciate the value of a rural road trip. A few are native daughters of small towns: Batavia, Cascade, Elkhart Lake, Greenbush, Hilbert, New Holstein, and beyond.

Globe Pequot

An imprint of Globe Pequot, the trade division of
The Rowman & Littlefield Publishing Group, Inc.
4501 Forbes Blvd., Ste. 200
Lanham, MD 20706
www.rowman.com

Distributed by NATIONAL BOOK NETWORK

British Library Cataloguing in Publication Information Available

Library of Congress Cataloging-in-Publication Data
Names: Bergin, Mary, 1955– author.
Title: Small-town Wisconsin : fun, surprising, and exceptional road trips / Mary Bergin.
Description: Essex, Connecticut : Globe Pequot, [2023] | Includes bibliographical references and index.
Identifiers: LCCN 2022046194 (print) | LCCN 2022046195 (ebook) | ISBN 9781493065943 (paperback) | ISBN 9781493065950 (epub)
Subjects: LCSH: Small cities—Wisconsin—Guidebooks. | Wisconsin—Description and travel.
Classification: LCC F579.3 .B48 2023 (print) | LCC F579.3 (ebook) | DDC 917.7504/44—dc23/eng/20221007
LC record available at https://lccn.loc.gov/2022046194
LC ebook record available at https://lccn.loc.gov/2022046195

♾™ The paper used in this publication meets the minimum requirements of American National Standard for Information Sciences—Permanence of Paper for Printed Library Materials, ANSI/NISO Z39.48-1992.

Front cover, clockwise from top: Canoe Bay Resort, Chetek; Cana Island Lighthouse, Baileys Harbor; Oktoberfest, New Glarus; The Clearing Folk School, Ellison Bay; Mill Pond, Wild Rose; Buena Vista Park, Alma. Back cover: (left) Wisconsin Great Northern Railroad, Spooner; (right) Duesterbeck's Brewing Company, Elkhorn

Contents

Wisconsin

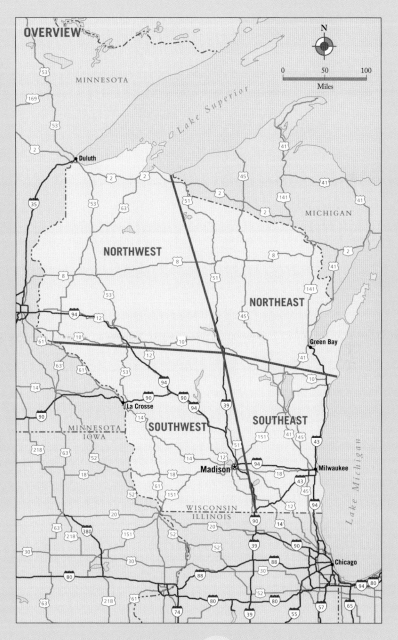

OVERVIEW

MINNESOTA

Lake Superior

Duluth

NORTHWEST

MICHIGAN

NORTHEAST

Green Bay

MINNESOTA
IOWA

SOUTHWEST

La Crosse

SOUTHEAST

Madison

Milwaukee

Lake Michigan

WISCONSIN
ILLINOIS

Chicago

N

0   50   100
Miles

Introduction

My life began in Hulls Crossing, a loosely knit farming community in northwest Sheboygan County. You won't find it on modern
maps. Little more than road signs survive as evidence.

Hulls Crossing was a railroad stop with depot in the late 1800s
until tracks were rerouted. One-teacher Hulls Crossing School, for
grades one through eight, closed after I finished first grade with
three classmates. Fire destroyed the lone nonfarm business—Hulls
Crossing Cheese Factory—in the early 1960s, a spectacular blaze
that I could almost feel from my bedroom window, one dip in the
road away.

So, the community's name faded with time and turned into a
cartographic phantom. What could have matured into a vibrant
hamlet got lost.

Today, the area is best known for wetlands restoration and
ecological diversity—an extension of Sheboygan Marsh Wildlife
Area that, happily, includes our converted farmland. The evolution
certainly is far more honorable than, say, being home to yet another Dollar Store or Starbucks.

That's my little story, and you have yours, too. The soul of who
we are as Wisconsinites—loyal, quirky, down to earth, humble—
takes root with how and where we are raised. For many, our earli-
est memories are of life in or near a small town.

Whether that community thrives, morphs, or vanishes from
one generation to the next depends on luck, finances, intention,
and will. This book features fifty examples of destinations with
something significant in character that defines and enriches their
location. Dozens of additional burgs are mentioned more briefly.

It takes something beyond having pretty parks or shoreline to make the cut: Wisconsin is home to a multitude of attractive hamlets. Appearance counts but isn't everything: a few locations might lack polish or sophistication yet preserve something uniquely noteworthy.

Consider this a selective look at places to visit for an hour or two, during a specific time of year, an overnight, or full-blown vacation. Link several of these little towns for a multiday road trip. You decide how to proceed.

I wanted to write this type of book because tourism promoters—with occasional exceptions—tend to bypass the tiniest in size among us. Most small towns don't have a huge, or any, marketing budget. They may not have a chamber of commerce or bother with much of a website. Community leaders work hard but quietly, with little time or interest in widespread outreach, fanfare, or posturing.

My first pitch for this book project was to take a best-of-the-Midwest U.S. approach, but my editor opted for one state at a time, beginning with my native Wisconsin. Smart advice. It challenged me to delve more deeply, beyond areas that already manage to generate a lot of attention.

Since 2002, I have been a Wisco-centric writer producing—at minimum—one weekly column/essay/blog and often seeking lesser-known destinations that are worthy of attention.

So, I figured that 10,000 was a reasonable population cutoff for this book.

It didn't take much research and organizing to decide that the Badger State has enough worthy destinations with fewer than 5,000 residents. Twenty of my fifty are under 1,000 in population, and that includes three spots—Custer, Genesee Depot, and Johnsonville—whose population is not tracked because they are not CDPs (census designated places).

It was a surprise to discover that a few other communities mentioned briefly but widely known to Wisconsinites—such as Fish Creek in Door County and Malone in Fond du Lac County—also are not CDPs.

U.S. Census Bureau data from 2020 is the source for population statistics, but the website only offers access to cities, towns, and villages with at least 5,000 population. My thanks go to Dan Barroilhet, demographer and research analyst at the Wisconsin Department of Administration, for providing spreadsheets so I could find info about much smaller communities. Some communities are in a township with the same name.

Dan estimates 1,678 municipalities in the state have fewer than 5,000 residents. That does not include CDPs, which the Census Bureau defines as "closely settled, unincorporated communities that are locally recognized and identified by name." The bureau recognizes CDPs "to provide meaningful statistics for well-known, unincorporated communities."

Interesting factoid: in Wisconsin, unincorporated communities aren't casually added to the state map, but anybody can submit a request. From the state cartographer's office: "The community should have either a dependable motorist service such as a service or repair garage, a major traffic attraction such as a consolidated school or major industry, or a recognized point of interest to which tourists might be regularly directed."

At least fifty people—"a reasonable permanent population"—must live in the vicinity. After all this info is verified, a practical point comes into play: there must be "adequate space" to add a new community name to the map.

As I write this, a front-page *Chicago Tribune* article reveals that many remote workers are moving to small towns that "better match their lifestyles as the pandemic reshapes the workplace."

Some small communities are proactive, offering financial and other incentives—via MakeMyMove.com—to persuade outsiders to move in and experience the sense of community that less-populated places aim to foster. The goal: revitalization through a renewal of energy/productivity and a more diverse demographic.

Has pandemic isolation, global strife, or polarizing politics changed your perspective about what makes life good, or where to live? Maybe one of these communities will turn into more than your next vacation getaway.

NOTE: Business hours and circumstances are ever-changing, so check for updates before you begin driving.

Southwest

Wherever you drift, on purpose or by instinct, expect to be surprised.

Follow the Great River Road, Highway 35, as it shadows the Mississippi and pay attention to often-weathered riverfront towns with endearing characters and a rich history.

Away from water is a pure joyride through our Driftless Area, the swath of Earth that glaciers bypassed thousands of years ago. Stunning hills, valleys, and rock formations remain because the area is unglaciated. So do coulees and bluffs, farm towns and orchards.

The quartzite cliffs of Devil's Lake, our most popular state park, are here. So are tiny towns with deep devotion to ethnic heritage and prolific farmers whose cranberry and apple production are nationally known and respected.

Watch for black buggies pulled by horses, too. Wisconsin's largest enclave of Amish farmers is hard at work in this part of the state.

Alma

Population 716

Castlerock Museum

castlerockmuseum.com
(608) 685-4231

Look what can happen when a 10-year-old boy pays $3 for a Civil War musket and decides he wants to learn more, more, and more. From curiosity sprouts a collection, then a passion, mission, and—in this case—specialty museum that rivals others of international repute.

Castlerock Museum is a self-guided walk through 2,000 years of curated history, the work of Gary Schlosstein, longtime Buffalo County Circuit Court judge. Interpretive panels and artwork put into context this collection of medieval and other antique arms and armor.

Arms such as a sword carried in the First Crusade (1095–1102). In the world are eight like it, but only on this one is a religious inscription, the names of Jesus and Mary in Latin.

Armor such as a complete, fluted Maximilian suit, a distinct style from the early 1500s that isn't as heavy as it appears. When acquired by Gary at an art auction, it was the first time the armor was sold since the early 1800s.

Add hundreds of additional artifacts, authentic and rare: Roman helmet and sword, Viking chieftain's sword, embossed Italian parade helmet, King Henry VIII gun shield, August the Strong boar spear.

Others—such as the Art Institute of Chicago—may have larger collections of arms and armor but keep much more in storage, say Gary and his executive director, Bill Wolcott. At least 90 percent of this nonprofit museum's holdings are on display, and historically accurate illustrations (photos, artwork reproductions) show the arms and armor being used.

"We try to tell a story here," the museum founder says. Other museums tend to categorize and separate: "The metal goes in one gallery, artwork in another." A part of the story shows the development and change of weaponry and science: "Much in science was driven by the development of weaponry" as a matter of survival and protection.

Art historian Christopher Dobson, former master armorer for the United Kingdom's royal armories, spent two weeks in little Alma to help Gary set up the museum, which opened in 2008. The two forged a friendship decades ago, through their mutual interest.

Most artifacts were acquired during Gary's trips abroad: "I traveled to Europe and learned a lot, which expanded my interest." He got to know major European and U.S. auction houses—Sotheby's,

FAST FIVE

Alma is 7 miles long but only two streets wide because of the location, between steep bluffs and the Mississippi River. Get a workout by walking "**stair step streets**" that connect Main and Second Streets. Still intact are eleven of these staircases.

Atop Alma's limestone bluffs is **Danzinger Vineyards**, whose eighteen acres of grapes turn into award winners at Minnesota and Wisconsin state fairs. Patio views can't be beat. danzingervineyard.com, (608) 685-6000

See the Mississippi River Valley from **Buena Vista Park**, 500 feet above Alma's downtown. The panoramic view, on a clear day, stretches several miles. Drive there or park downtown and follow a Second Street hiking trail to the top.

Catch bass, catfish, sunfish, or walleye at the **Great Alma Fish Float**, near the Mississippi's Lock and Dam No. 4. To get there, find the chipped red bench at riverside and pull up a hinged slab of painted wood. That lets the float operator know you need a ride over. Open seasonally.

Nature meets art at **Wings Over Alma**, a nonprofit in an 1880 building that aims to raise awareness of regional artists and Upper Mississippi environment.

Think nature talks and art exhibits. wingsoveralma.org, (608) 685-3303

For more: explorealma.com, (608) 685-4935.

Christie's, beyond—and learned which dealers would be most reliable in ascertaining authenticity. "Major auction houses make sure that what you're acquiring is authentic," he notes. "They have their honor on the line."

Bill says the two-story museum—castle-like in appearance—is expanding to add two American history galleries for almost 250 items from Colonial America through World War II.

"We're getting better known," Bill says; a western U.S. collector donated to Castlerock his collection of fifty antique swords, helmets, and daggers. Travelers from around the world discover Alma because of the museum: one of the first visitors was from Vietnam.

Why Alma? Gary is from the area, and the courthouse where he was circuit judge for 36 years is across the street. In the city is a National Historic District of 200-plus buildings.

What does the museum still need? "I'll know it when I see it," he says. "Collecting is like love—it never ends."

Cashton

Population 1,158

Growers Produce Auction

growersproduceauction.com
(608) 654-7880

"Let's go fifty, a dollar-fifty. Now two. And fifty. Now three. And fifty, just fifty—do we have three-fifty? Fifty?

"Sold, for three dollars. All right, times forty-five . . ."

Yikes. Had I just bought forty-five double impatiens for $135? Or did he say "four or five," whatever I wanted?

Neither. The auctioneer was just rushing into his next sing-song of bids, for flats of smaller flowers. My purchase was "times twelve"—which means I bought a dozen near-identical plants. The foot-tall flowers were lush, fat with blossoms.

No two auctioneers sound exactly alike, but their lyrical, rhythmic riffs are the kind of serenade that could rival rap musicians. The lilt seems hypnotic, and this is a part of what turns a Growers Produce Auction into a memorable event.

AMISH 101

When traveling through Amish countryside and communities, drive slowly and keep a respectful distance from horse-driven buggies.

Resist the temptation to stare or photograph Amish people; they are private and modest people who do not want to be treated like a sideshow.

Amish businesses are not open on Sundays because it is a day of worship.

For information about the Amish in the United States, consult amishamerica.com.

Amish families in southwest Wisconsin sell their products here at least twice weekly during summer, but Memorial Day and Labor Day sales are bigger.

Merchandise—thousands of potted flowers and vegetables, dozens of hand-stitched quilts, hand-carved furniture, and myriad other crafts—fills and spills out of an otherwise stark, metal warehouse on the two holidays. It is enough to keep three auctioneers busy about 8 hours.

Customers are average people, professional chefs and wholesale buyers for grocery stores or restaurants. At a smaller auction in late summer, sisters loaded up on potted mums as décor for an outdoor wedding. A buyer who drove 5 hours would return with enough veggies to stock roadside stands in Door County.

Another bought bushels of corn as bear bait. A home canner bought a peck of pickles. A hodgepodge mix of tomatoes and peppers was destined to become salsa and pepper jam.

Most vendors are farm families within a radius of one hundred miles; they rise before dawn to gather and deliver the bounty of hard labor. Auction staff say these farms are not big enough for most wholesalers.

As crops ripen, farmers will tote more bushels of just-picked food than ready-to-plant shrubs and flower flats. Harvests are sold in quantities that often exceed—by far—the needs of a typical household.

Dozens of horses hitched to black buggies slowly and methodically transport commodities to the rural sales site for auction on Tuesdays and Fridays, April into October. The time it takes depends on how much is for sale.

Not all who witness the refrains of auctioneers and sashay of bidders are buyers: wanderers come for good deals and good quality, yes, but also for an introduction to what it means to be Amish. Within Wisconsin are about 15,000 Amish residents (fourth largest in the nation), and the Cashton settlement is the state's biggest.

"This truly is an Old Order community," says Kathy Kuderer, founder of **Down a Country Road** shops and tours near Cashton. "They have stayed very true to their horse-and-buggy culture and still do not use electricity, have telephones in their homes, or heat their homes with propane." downacountryroad.com, (608) 654-5318

That means using gas or kerosene lanterns for light and a woodstove for cooking and warmth. "Ice is cut from the area ponds in the winter, for their ice houses," says Kathy, who was raised in the area, "and all of the field work is done with horse-drawn equipment."

Amish products are sold within a cluster of her shops. Guided tours (by reservation) began decades ago and stop at Amish farms in this part of pretty southwestern Wisconsin, where hilly and twisting roads force visitors to remove themselves from life's fast lane for a while. A map with self-guided tour book is another option.

Simple, wooden roadside signs advertise bounty or craftsmanship—such as bakery, porch furniture—but don't swing into a driveway unless serious about making a purchase. These hardworking families prefer to not be interrupted by gawking tourists.

WORTHY DETOUR

Friends near Cazenovia, population 363, traditionally invite us to their farm as spring turns to summer, and it is a joy to simply follow quiet, twisty backroads to their home on a hill with unobstructed, sweeping views of fields, wildlife, and passing clouds. It's about 40 miles southwest of Cashton.

We usually share a potluck meal and, maybe, a game of washers or cornhole. We sit on the porch, spoil the farm cats, smell the lilacs, and watch orioles swoop in for a quick peck at a feeder with jelly.

This annual ritual begins with shopping—all within a 5-mile loop of Lime Ridge, population 158—and anticipation begins weeks ahead of our arrival.

We order cinnamon-topped and cream-filled coffee cakes, gooey pans of pecan rolls, pies, cookies, and more from **Esther's Bakery**, an Amish home business only open on Friday and Saturday. Those who don't order ahead will take their chances because bakery disappears fast.

Because there is no website, email, or telephone, the only way to place an order is by knowing somebody who will relay it. That's also the case at **Sugar Grove Candy Shoppe**, which sells chocolate toffee, cashew brittle, and other sweets.

The oldest **Carr Valley Cheese** factory (open since 1902) is in our loop, near La Valle, population 388. The most likely purchase is made-that-day cheese curds, but the fourth-generation business makes numerous cheeses that have won 750-some international, national, and other awards. carrvalleycheese.com, (608) 985-8200

Late spring is planting season for much of Wisconsin, so we load up on flats and baskets at **Gingerich Greenhouse**, an Amish business with reasonable prices and healthy stock.

Need more ideas or directions? Talk it over during lunch at **Branding Iron Roadhouse** in Lime Ridge, serving Wisconsin microbrews, burgers from locally grown Angus beef, Neapolitan pizzas from a wood-fired oven. brandingironrh.com, (608) 986-2807

Particularly picturesque and serene are 17 miles of Highway D, from Cashton to La Farge, population 730. Notice clotheslines full of blue, black, and white laundry, windmills atop vistas, the lack of power lines, noise, or clutter. Look for Old Country Cheese, a factory whose gift shop sells Amish specialties as well as dairy products made with the milk of 230 Amish farms. oldcountrycheese.com, (608) 654-5411

At the end of this route is headquarters for Organic Valley, among the largest farming cooperatives in the United States; a small, downtown retail outlet for the co-op sells these and other products. organicvalley.coop, (608) 625-3300

Gays Mills

Population 523

Apple Orchards

orchardridgegaysmills.com

We call them Ocooch Mountains, but they're more like steep bluffs, and this modest village sits in a valley between them. Farmers learned long ago that apples grow well here, and the literal fruits of their labors earned a national reputation for taste and appearance.

FAST FACT

Crawford County was fertile fodder for native son Ben Logan, who wrote *The Land Remembers*, tender tales of growing up on a farm that his mother called Seldom Seen. He moved to New York to work in radio, television, and movie writing/production but never forgot his roots and returned to Seldom Seen in the 1980s. Ben, who won an Emmy for his work on the 1986 documentary *Taking Children Seriously*, died in 2014 at age 94.

"Once you have lived on the land, been a partner with its moods, secrets, and seasons, you cannot leave," he wrote in the 1975 book. "The living land remembers, touching you in unguarded moments, saying, 'I am here. You are part of me.'"

Mississippi Valley Conservancy worked with the author to make sure Seldom Seen will remain as farmland and organizes occasional hikes in this part of Wisconsin. mississippivalleyconservancy.org, (608) 784-3606

Apples from local orchards were gathered as one State Fair entry, winning first prize. Next came a national competition and another top prize. The year was 1905.

Almost four dozen kinds of apples grow on more than 1,000 acres in the area today. Six commercial orchards along Highway 171, known as "Orchard Ridge," make for a stunning drive. That's especially true during three days in late September, when tens of thousands visit for the annual Gays Mills Apple Festival, in the Apple Capital of Wisconsin.

Festival days begin with a pancake-sausage breakfast and end with bands that play rock or country music at area taverns. In between are volleyball, basketball, cornhole, and horseshoe tournaments. A parade with festival royalty in gowns and tiaras. Vendors selling crafts, books, antiques, and trash-to-treasure items.

Apple'licious Pie Depot tries valiantly to keep up with the demand for just-baked pie, streusel, fritters, turnovers, doughnuts, and apple pizza with a topping of caramel. On Facebook, (608) 624-3783

Pack your patience for the long wait in orchard checkout lines, or simply visit another day to roam and buy. The apple harvest starts in August and ends in October; specifics depend on the weather and type of apple.

Buy by the bag or bushel. Add a jug of cider. Linger in a corn maze or at an orchard café table.

DECENT DETOUR

Seven miles north is Soldiers Grove, population 552, and the **Tobacco Warehouse Inn**, a renovated 1923 warehouse with six suites of classy accommodations that would rival those in much larger cities. tobaccowarehouse inn.com, (608) 624-5999

Between the two communities is **St. Francis Hermitage Restaurant**, where a monastic community serves French meals and sells organic vegetables and meats from their farm. Think crepes with paper-thin apple slices, flaky croissants, brioche bread, French press coffee.

Consider it an appetizing apparition that appears out of nowhere. The religious community also built a charming little church on the rural property. stfrancis hermitage.org, (608) 735-4015

The fertile ground of Gays Mills is prone to flooding. To say the Kickapoo River, which runs through the community, is crooked is an understatement. Fewer than 70 miles separate one end point from the other, but it's 125 miles by river. Erosion from higher ground compounds the effect of heavy rain.

Troubled waters—the foundation for a turbulent history—devastated much of the village and prompted the relocation of dozens of houses and businesses to higher, safer ground. Two major flash floods, in 2007 and 2008, were only ten months apart. Flooding since then has been even more significant and in 2018 went much higher than ever recorded.

What we have is tempestuous beauty, in a small community big enough to have a village forester who leads the charge against emerald ash borer consequences and trees damaged or destroyed by flooding. An ongoing Urban Forestry Program recognizes the multipronged value of adding trees and keeping them healthy.

"Our community trees provide significant health-promoting, eco-logical, economic and aesthetic benefits," village president Harry Heisz noted in 2021, when declaring May 1 as Arbor Day. A self-guided tree walk goes through Robb Park, then south along Stump Dodger Trail. gaysmills.org, (608) 735-4341

Mineral Point

Population 2,581

First Historic District

**mineralpoint.com
(608) 987-3201**

Mineral Point visionaries long ago began to see something beautiful in what others presumed disposable.

The hardscrabble lead mining town of Cornish immigrants during the 1800s is a magnet for artists and others who appreciate a blend of past with present today. Many work out of the 500-some buildings that compose a historic district—Wisconsin's first—on the National Register of Historic Places since 1971.

Little of the transformation would have happened without the work of Edgar Hellum and Robert Neal, who saw cultural value in stone homes that miners abandoned in their rush to find gold in California.

The business and life partners began restoring the little cottages in the 1930s, named one Pendarvis and turned it into a restaurant for

serving tea and saffron cake, then pasties (meat-potato pies) and more. The couple did it all, baking to roof shingling, and drew attention from *Life, National Geographic, the Saturday Evening Post,* and others.

Food critic Duncan Hines, best known for food products named after him, included Pendarvis in his *Adventures in Good Eating* guidebooks. "One of the few places in this country where real Cornish meals are served, prepared from old authentic recipes, and where scalded cream (often called Devonshire or clotted cream) may be had," he wrote. Pasties "must be ordered four hours in advance" but are "hearty and appetizing."

The duo's knack for cooking, decorating, and building rehab was ridiculed by some townsfolk, but others eventually began their own restoration efforts. Projects snowballed, and now a city Historic Preservation Commission reviews architectural changes to historic buildings and drafts guidelines for these endeavors.

Pendarvis, no longer a restaurant, is a state historic site of restored buildings with walking trails to mine shafts and "badger holes"—hillside caves that were miner shelters and resembled animal burrows. Wisconsin is the Badger State because of the once-rich mining history here and elsewhere. Open June into October for guided tours. pendarvis .wisconsinhistory.org, (608) 987-2122

A short walk away is Shake Rag Alley Art Center, another example of rugged history in need of TLC. Al Felly, a longtime and nationally known florist, in 1965 purchased a Mineral Point house as a retreat for him and his wife. Five years later, he bought rundown limestone cabins, across the street, and began restoring them for artists to use. Flower gardens grew lush, too.

By 2004, the campus was a nonprofit arts education hub and had different owners. Now it hosts more than 200 workshops for adults and youths annually, plus free or nominal-cost community events.

An original one-room Cornish cottage, 1830 log cabin, blacksmith barn, and more modern structures make for an unusual campus that expanded to include an outdoor performance stage, repurposed 1940s

Quonset hut, and accommodations for overnight stays.

Students come for a day or week to paint, weave, weld, write, throw a pot, or bake a galette.

Like the city's visionaries, some workshop participants turn castoff materials into works of artistic beauty. That is especially true at the annual Woodlanders Gathering, a summer camp for adults that can last one to four days.

Novices to pros make their way here to get in touch with themselves, each other, and the Earth while learning or refining art skills.

They create yard art, rustic furniture, jewelry and scarves, using twigs, stones, metals, fabric. Natural dyes, roaring fires, hammers and nails transform the ordinary to the unique. Myriad materials are involved, and they also result in leather journals, bluebird houses, fancy walking sticks, coat trees, garden sculptures, or whimsical art with no utilitarian purpose.

Hang out in a class long enough, and you may hear an orchestra of tools, a mix of hammering, sawing, and the smooth slide of metal measuring tape. Parents attend with their teen children. Girlfriends arrive in groups. Some students enroll solo.

Some of these gatherings include silent "trade blanket" time, when participants bring whatever they are willing to let go of, then take something brought by another.

It's an exercise in giving, receiving, and reinforcing the notion of what contains value in this world.

shakeragalley.org, (608) 987-3292

IN THE NEIGHBORHOOD

Built into a Mineral Point hill is the stone and forty-two-room **Walker House**, constructed in 1836. Nooks in the inn's pub were the long-ago dugout caves of miners. The comfortable retreat space also serves from-scratch pasties, soups, desserts, and is a few steps from the 47-mile Cheese Country Trail, a multiuse rec path. thewalkerhouse.org, (608) 553-0728

Downstairs at **Commerce Street Brewery Hotel** is a brewpub serving Blonde Betty II (named after actress Betty White) to wash down jalapeño-spiked cheese curds (with raspberry sauce for dipping). Upstairs are plush guest rooms with a fireplace and modern amenities. The setting: a revamped 1854 limestone warehouse. commercehotel.com, (608) 987-3298

A bag of squeaky-fresh cheese curds from **Hooks Cheese Company** is an in-demand and affordable souvenir, but the downtown cheesemaker wins national and international awards for at least fifteen other products. hookscheese.com, (608) 987-3259

Roam **Nick Engelbert's Grandview**, near Hollandale (population 306), a dairy farmer's legacy as a self-taught artist. Over thirty years he created dozens of concrete statues and embellished his farmhouse and yard with shards of random materials. nicksgrandview.com, (608) 967-2122

Folklore Village, 94 acres surrounded by farmland and hills, hosts one hundred events annually that celebrate heritage. Waltz on hardwood floors, listen to folk artists and autoharps, weave maypole ribbons into patterns, learn rosemaling or gourd banjo making. The vibe is downhome—as in Saturday night potlucks—and family friendly. folklorevillage.com, (608) 924-4000

Closest state parks: Three are within 15 miles. To the north: **Governor Dodge**, one of the state's largest. To the southwest: **Belmont Mound**, whose best views are atop a 400-foot hill. Southeast is **Yellowstone Lake**, part of a state wildlife area. dnr.wisconsin.gov

New Glarus

Population 2,266

Swiss Center of North America

theswisscenter.org
(608) 527-6565

More than one-half century before New Glarus became a village, the community was a Swiss colony of immigrants who were literally starving for work. With widespread crop failures came famine in their native land.

Switzerland's canton of Glarus, similar to a U.S. state, helped one hundred-some citizens start fresh as they emigrated to the beautiful but wild New World in 1845. Here they could work to own land; the woods and hills of where they landed were reminders of home.

What separates this story of immigration from others is the zest with which culture, history, and lore are joyfully—perhaps stubbornly—upheld. In "America's Little Switzerland" is a *männerchor* (men's choir), *kinderchor* (youth choir), and *jodlerklub* (choir of yodelers). Out come meters-long alphorns (used long ago by Swiss to call cattle home) during festivals.

IN THE NEIGHBORHOOD

Ten miles south of New Glarus is the rural **Chalet Cheese Coopera- tive**, around since 1885 and the only cheese factory in the nation that produces pungent and creamy Limburger cheese, one of the smelliest cheeses on Earth. How aromatic? It is wrapped in a paper-plastic, then foil. Buy it at the cheese factory, along with a chunk of Deppeler's Baby Swiss, an international award winner. chaletcheesecoop.com, (608) 325-4343

Seven miles northeast is Belleville, population 2,491, and an outlet for **Duluth Trading Company** sells fashions for work-hard men and women at a deep discount. duluthtrading.com, (608) 424-1227

Twelve miles northeast is Paoli, where **Seven Acre Dairy** revives a century-old creamery's work and adds bou- tique lodging, fine din- ing. Pack lawn chairs in summer and head to craft brewer **Hop Garden**, next to Paoli Mill Park on the Sugar River, where free music on weekends is life as usual. En route, check out **Dot's Tavern**, a basement dive bar and top reason to visit Basco, especially if a meat raffle is in progress. Neither blip of a community is a census des- ignated place. sevenacredairyco.com, thehopgarden.net, discoverpaoli.com; Dot's is on Facebook.

Southeast 25 miles is **Kelch Aviation Museum** at the airport in Brodhead, population 3,274, where nineteen vin- tage aircraft include the only Butler Blackhawk still airworthy. This one is from 1929, as is the Stearman C3-8. Add three classic autos, interactive exhibits. Free admission. kelchmuseum.org

"Our mission is to tell the story of Swiss immigration in the United States and Canada," says Beth Zurbuchen, president/CEO of the Swiss Center of North America. "What better place to be than New Glarus, which works hard to maintain its Swissness. There are many communities either settled by the Swiss or those that have a Swiss name, but over time" uniqueness of heritage blends into a more generic melting pot known as American.

At the crux of holdings are Don Tritt's historical archives, which include thousands of Swiss postcards from 1895 to 1945 and stereoviews (three-dimensional images) from 1860 to 1940. Add Swiss textiles, fine and folk art, musical instruments, home furnishings, books, family genealogies.

"If it's of Swiss origin, it is our desire to obtain and keep the items from being given away to thrift stores or thrown away," Beth says, and the potential for doing so is especially rich in this little part of the world.

"In New Glarus, families followed settlers. Farmers or cheesemakers could find work. Men who became financially secure returned to Switzerland to find their brides and return back to New Glarus to begin their families." Pride of place deepened with time.

"Each item, story, or manuscript helps enrich our understanding of the Swiss immigration to North America."

Inside **Swiss Historical Village** are fourteen structures—replicas and originals—with artifacts that explain the challenges of pioneer life. **Chalet of the Golden Fleece**, an authentic Swiss chalet, protects one man's many collections of antiques and folk art (including items from his Swiss ancestry). Both open late May into October. swisshistoricalvillage.org, (608) 527-2317; chalet is on Facebook, (608) 527-2614.

Open car windows during a summer drive and listen for the tinkling of bells worn by Brown Swiss cows as they graze. Inside **Puempel's**, a

FAST FACT

Spotted Cow is the flagship beer at New Glarus Brewing Company, whose "Only in Wisconsin" slogan means products are sold only inside the state. That creates an almost cultlike following for the product, an unfiltered farmhouse ale, brewed to meet German Purity Law brewing standards.

The brewer's assertion that "You know you're in Wisconsin when you see the Spotted Cow" is no understatement: because this love-it beer is not available everywhere, it creates deep devotion within Wisconsin. Tour and taste. newglarusbrewing.com, (608) 527-5850

FAST FIVE

Consider a farm stay while in south-central Wisconsin. For example:

Campo di Bella, Dane County, rents a suite above its wine house. The 20-acre destination is one part farm, one part winery, and one part farm-to-table dining. campodibella.com, (608) 320-9287

Learn to milk a goat or spin fibers at 20-acre **Circle M Farm**, Lafayette County, then retreat to the cozy confines of a "glamper"—revamped camper from the 1950s. Soak in steam from the farm's private sauna. circlemfarm.com, (608) 636-4652

Inn Serendipity, Green County, is a 5-acre organic farm that is totally powered by renewable energy. Ride a recumbent bike that generates electricity while pedaling. The bed-and-breakfast is a showcase for sustainable living. innserendipity.com, (608) 329-7056

A fourth generation operates **Wegmueller Farm's** 500 acres and dairy cattle in Green County. Get acquainted through the *Farm for Thought* podcast. Stay in the remodeled four-bedroom and two-bath farmhouse. farmforthought.org, (608) 325-7356

Several farms in the area are operated by women who unite as **Soil Sisters** to host an annual weekend of farm tours, workshops, and culinary events in August. soilsisterswi.org

Not a working farm but on 120 acres: **Cameo Rose Victorian Country Inn**, a rural estate that has won numerous awards for accommodations and breakfasts (think Banana Split Muffins, French Hot Cocoa Supreme). cameorose.com, (608) 424-6340

tavern since 1893 and immigrant-era boardinghouse, are murals of the motherland and occasional card games of jass. puempels.com, (608) 527-2045

Throughout the village is an all-year "cow parade" (fifteen life-sized cow sculptures painted by artists), alpine chalet architecture, and Swiss flags. The 1910 New Glarus Bakery makes marzipan-filled almond horns and walnut-rich nut horns. Dine on fondues and schnitzels at Chalet Landhaus. newglarusbakery.com, (608) 527-2916; chaletlandhaus.com, (608) 527-5234

The annual Heidi Festival, since the 1960s, diverts attention to the legendary Swiss shepherdess in late June. The fight to free Switzerland from Austrian rule is at the heart of Wilhelm Tell Festival performances, which began in 1938 and fill Labor Day weekend. New is Silvesterchlausen, a procession of yodelers in costume, toting bells to ring in a new year.

For more about the area: swisstown.com, (608) 527-2095.

Potosi

Population 646

ABA National Brewery Museum

potosibrewery.com
(608) 763-4002

Along the Great River Road, which follows the Mississippi nearly 3,000 miles, are big cities known for iconic architecture (Gateway Arch in St. Louis), music (Graceland/Elvis in Memphis), and cuisine (Creole/Cajun in New Orleans).

Potosi is a David versus Goliath example of how the underdog fights successfully to make a name for itself, too. The little town beat out St. Louis and Milwaukee for the American Breweriana Association's first museum, open since 2008.

FAST FACT

Ripley's Believe It or Not noticed Potosi in the 1940s and decided it had the longest Main Street without an intersection. The community is sandwiched between two bluffs. Main Street ends at the 240,000-acre Upper Mississippi River Refuge, a national wildlife area.

The nonprofit association chose Potosi for the $7 million project because of the village's long brewing history and confidence that residents would see the project through.

Location is the four-story, 1852 Potosi Brewing Company Beer was made and shipped throughout the United States until the brewery closed in 1972. The museum project revived the business.

"We're fortunate this building was still standing," says Frank Fiorenza, retired village president. "It looked war-torn, but the foundation was still solid."

Also in the building are Potosi Brewing Company Transportation Museum, a Great River Road interpretive center, national brewery reference library, gift shop, and family-friendly brewpub. Open since 2015 is a modern brewhouse, new construction that boosted brewing capacity to 80,000 barrels per year.

Tapped spring water turns into twenty styles of Potosi beverages—Good Old Potosi (a pilsner), Snake Hollow IPA, hard seltzers, and a root beer—for starters. (Snake Hollow is a reference to when rattlesnakes were found in mining caves locally.)

In the brewpub, Potosi beer is a frequent recipe ingredient. Manager Konrad Arnold says beer goes into a cheese dip for Bavarian pretzels and into beer cheese soup. In barbecue sauce is Tangerine IPA. Pulled pork and corned beef will stew in Cave Ale.

Watch for "innovation batches" on tap—experiments in brewing—for customers to taste and offer feedback. "We usually ask them to choose between two—whichever they like best," Arnold says, and clear winners gain wider exposure.

During warm weather, an outdoor beer garden opens near a spring-fed koi pond. Free music and beer tours are booked on weekends. An annual beer festival, on the fourth Saturday of August, highlights in-house and other beer made in the region.

Museum artifacts come from hundreds of private collections, including those of the association's 3,000 members. The museum and library aim to serve historians, collectors, and the public.

At least 2,000 vintage television and radio commercials about beer are archived in the research library. So are rare books about brewing and oral history interviews about the industry.

What might you see at the museums? Depends on the visit: ABA members meet at the museum often to clean and add or subtract from displays, as new items are donated or items on loan are returned. americanbreweriana.org

HISTORICAL MARKER

Fifteen miles north of Potosi, on Highway 35 at Slabtown Road, is a state historical marker for **Pleasant Ridge**, a Black farming community of free and escaped slaves who arrived in the mid-1800s.

They built one of the nation's first integrated schools in 1873 and owned almost 700 acres of farmland by 1895, but subsequent generations left to seek opportunities elsewhere. Only the marker and a Black cemetery 1 mile west on Slabtown remain.

FRUIT OF THE VINE

Southwest Wisconsin Wine Trail weaves up, down, and around the Upper Mississippi River Valley. Four wineries occasionally cohost weekends that match their products with chocolate, cheese, or sausage.

These vintners ferment cold-hardy grapes, other fruits, or honey to make their beverages. On the often-rural route are **Spurgeon Vineyards**, Highland; **Sinnipee Valley Vineyard**, Cuba City; **Whispering Bluffs** and **Twisted Vines**, both in Potosi. southwestwisconsinwinetrail.com

FAITH-BASED DUO

Eight miles southeast of Potosi is **Dickeyville Grotto**, a campus of religious shrines built by a Catholic priest from 1925 to 1930. Stones and various gemstones, fossils, and castoff materials are embedded in concrete outside of Holy Ghost Church in Dickeyville, population 1,015. Donations appreciated. dickeyville grotto.com, (608) 568-3119

Ten more miles south is **Sinsinawa Mound Center**, whose Dominican sisters provide space for guided and private retreats. The on-site bakery is known for from-scratch breads and caramel rolls. sinsinawa.org, (608) 748-4415

DECENT DETOUR

Public shuttles by boat are increasingly rare along the Mississippi River, and some people drive hours to take a 17-minute ride on the seasonal **Pride of Cassville** ferry, which links Wisconsin and Iowa. It is 18 miles northwest of Potosi.

"We get people from all over the world," says deckhand Don Zahurance, who works part-time on the ferry and also is pastor at River Valley Community Church in Cassville, population 777.

The minister calls the car ferry "a moving monument" on what he describes as the narrowest and deepest part of the Mississippi. Ferry service began there in 1833 via a flatboat that was oared back and forth. Then horses on a treadmill powered the ferry until the animals were replaced by gas engines around 1912.

Cassville had no ferry service from 1942 to 1982, but then the village revived operations. Now Captain Kim Kottke hauls up to 98 tons per ride, up to thirty times per day, and has enough room to carry nine to fourteen vehicles at a time (or two semitrailers).

Most travelers rely on about 130 bridges between the river's end points of Lake Itasca in Minnesota and the Gulf of Mexico near New Orleans. Cassville's ferry season usually begins in May, but the start date might be postponed until midsummer because of high water. Service tends to end by early November.

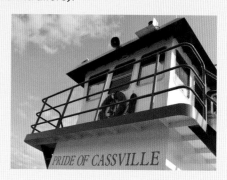

On an average summer weekday, passengers encounter little wait to board this shortcut to the Great River Road National Scenic Byway, on either side of the river. "Looping the loop" from ferry to road to bridge (as close as Marquette, Iowa, 60 miles north, and Dubuque, 35 miles south) is popular, especially among motorcyclists. Others opt to park and walk on for a quicker roundtrip ride.

Ride near sunset, and it will look like the sun sets in the north, but that is only because this bend of the Mississippi River runs east-west. Call the 24-hour information line to make sure the schedule is not affected by river conditions. cassville.org, (608) 725-5180

Closest state park: **Nelson Dewey**, on a bluff that is 500 feet above the Mississippi and home to Native American burial mounds. The park's 756 acres were in the late governor's 2,000-acre rural estate. dnr.wisconsin.gov

I've seen rare, pre-Prohibition brewing equipment, long stored in a Wisconsin farm shed. Lots of little things, too: beer cans and glasses, ad materials, other collectibles.

Unusual tales revolve around the Potosi Steamer, which until 1917 delivered pony kegs to Dubuque via the river while quenching the thirst of one hundred passengers. "Potosi's rolling bar, for thirty years," Frank explains. "It was the bar that came to you."

An elongated 1929 Pontiac was big enough for six bartenders to work out of at once and a popular rental unit for weddings. It had no liquor license, so you couldn't sell beer from it, but you could give it away. The vehicle was found abandoned in a field.

Roxbury

Population 1,871

Dorf Haus

foodspot.com
(608) 643-3980

Authentic Bavarian recipes, generations old. Commissioned paintings and stained-glass windows. In business since 1961, surrounded by farmland.

This is Dorf Haus, where prep for German potato salad still begins by hand-peeling potatoes. "Most of what we do is from scratch—soups,

spaetzle, stuffing," says Rebecca Maier-Frey, managing partner with her brother, Monte Maier. "The authenticity is extremely important to us in a day and age where people are getting it less and less."

Generations continue to find their way here for wedding receptions, postfuneral meals, holiday parties, fish on Fridays, and authentic German dishes all year. The only other major draw is St. Norbert's Catholic Parish, across the street.

The venture began by selling $1 family-style chicken dinners on weekends, twenty-five customers at a time. That was an experiment for Vern and Betty Maier, who bought the building where their wedding reception was held in 1950 and named it Dorf Haus—"the village inn."

Now "The Dorf" seats up to 450 and is the Maiers' legacy. The parents of nine children died twenty-two days apart in 2012, but the family's younger generation upholds the sense and taste of Bavaria that their parents deeply established.

"Our father loved to give tours—he was so proud of their collections—and we are so proud to keep telling the stories" behind the antiques-rich décor. One example: paintings, all depictions of King Ludwig's castles and countryside, were created by a local artist and a local priest.

FAST FACT

Twelve miles northwest of Roxbury, next to Delaney's Surplus but hidden from highway view, is **Dr. Evermor's Park**, all about trash-to-treasure scrapyard sculptures. Biggest is the **Forevertron**, 50 feet tall and 300 tons, created in the 1980s. worldofevermor.com, (608) 219-7830

ACROSS THE RIVER

Roxbury is 3 miles east of the Wisconsin River; across the waterway is the Sauk Prairie area. Although there is no such community, the name is a popular reference to Sauk City, population 3,518, and Prairie du Sac, population 4,420—communities so close that they seem like one. saukprairie.com, (608) 643-4168

Most unusual is the **Wisconsin State Cow Chip Throw**, a part of Labor Day weekend since 1975. Dried cow dung is flung by kids, adults, and corporate teams. The record, set in 1991 by Greg Neumaier, is 248 feet; this local resident won the competition seven consecutive years.

Chip chuckers choose their cow chips from a wagon loaded by the Meadow Muffin Committee. The cow chip became the state's Unofficial State Muffin in 1989. It's all in good fun (and the cow pies don't stink or stick because they are dried). wiscowchip.com, (608) 235-8193

Popular in winter is **Bald Eagle Watching Days**, mid-January, when knowledgeable, raptor-loving volunteers use videos and real-time observations of the birds to educate two-legged visitors. ferrybluff eaglecouncil.org

Good all year is **Wollersheim Winery**, where hillside vineyards began producing grapes in the 1840s. The farm was restored to a working winery in the 1970s. By 1989, Wollersheim gained national attention for its Prairie Fumé, a semidry white and triple-gold medalist that is Wisconsin's most popular wine.

An expansion added a distillery for brandy and other spirits. A lunchtime bistro serves sandwiches, salads, soups, and snacks. Visit for the Port Celebration in January, Ruby Nouveau Release Day in November, or another time to tour, taste, and nibble while absorbing the quiet scenery. wollersheim.com, (800) 847-9463

Follow the Wisconsin River 10 miles northeast to Merrimac, population 527, for the fun of crossing the waterway on a free, **fifteen-car ferry** that typically operates mid-April through November. It is the state's only free ferry; the crossing links Highway 113 and takes 7 minutes. Service began in the 1840s, and cables pull the ferry across the lake. wisconsin dot.gov, (608) 246-3872

Those early-year chicken dinners remain on the menu, but so do traditional German entrées and standard supper club fare. Popular appetizers are chicken livers and huge, soft pretzels.

On Fridays during Lent, turtle meat is marinated overnight with carrots and onions, roasted four hours, and served with mashed potatoes, coleslaw, and fritters. The novelty began in the 1980s because Catholic customers wanted a legit option to fish. Orders are phoned in advance, so supply matches demand.

Oldest recipes? One for stuffing dates back multiple generations. The recipe for sauerbraten "was shared with our parents by one of their first cooks—she was 100 percent German."

"The great thing about Roxbury is that it has not changed much since we were young kids," Rebecca says. "A few more houses, but still a small village tucked into the rolling hills of southern Wisconsin."

On a Thanksgiving with no need to cook, my guy and I drove to Dorf Haus and naively expected a modest number of diners because of the pandemic. Wrong—although the restaurant had scaled back on reservations, it still served 560 guests (instead of the usual 700-some). Donated that day was $3,000 in restaurant proceeds to help fight pancreatic cancer.

"Mom started it when she was diagnosed," Rebecca says. "We will continue donations, in her memory."

Similarly, Monday is typically a slow night for dining, but that wasn't the case at Dorf Haus, which historically hosted a smorgasbord at least monthly, and it turned into one big party. A polka band performed from an elevated stage, above a wooden dance floor.

On the buffet were Bavarian favorites: schnitzels, sauerbraten, *schweinsrippen*, knackwurst, pork hocks, spaetzle, kraut, braised red cabbage, salads, and desserts. The pandemic and supply chain issues interrupted the tradition.

To come: an expanded biergarten because "we have a beautiful setting that we love to share with our friends."

Spring Green

Population 1,566

Taliesin

taliesinpreservation.org
(608) 588-7900

"Sacred space." That is what I scrawled in a notebook shortly after spring's arrival in 2019. The phrase most often is associated with a house of worship, but not on this day. Neither was it a sanctuary of the natural world.

I was lingering inside Taliesin, the rural estate where Frank Lloyd Wright worked and lived. Got up close to artifacts that still make the place feel like home. Heard curators' backstories about the structure and furnishings. Sat with my private thoughts, on a comfy chair next to a bronze bust of the legendary architect.

Four months later, this property and seven others by Wright were designated a UNESCO World Heritage Site, a move that acknowledged "outstanding universal value"—as in international significance—and placed Taliesin in elite company internationally.

Think Taj Mahal in India, Giza pyramids in Egypt, Eiffel Tower in France. This is the company that Taliesin keeps as a World Heritage Site.

The fabled architect's work "goes far beyond the boundaries of the United States of America," a UNESCO committee wrote. Wright's twentieth-century designs "strongly impacted on the development of modern architecture" globally. UNESCO described him as "one of the most influential architects of his century."

TRAILING WRIGHT LANDMARKS

Among Frank Lloyd Wright's designs are twenty-six National Historic Landmarks, including six in Wisconsin:

Taliesin (a landmark since 1976)

S. C. Johnson Administration Building and Research Tower, Racine (1976)

Wingspread, Racine (1989)

Herbert and Katherine Jacobs First House, Madison (2003)

Herbert and Katherine Jacobs Second House, Madison (2003)

First Unitarian Society Meeting House, Madison (2004)

For details: nps.gov.

In Wisconsin is a 250-mile, self-guided Frank Lloyd Wright trail that leads to his designs in nine counties. Download a trail app at wrightinwisconsin.org.

Of Wright's 1,114 architectural designs, each of his eight World Heritage locations "has specific characteristics, representing new solutions to the needs for housing, worship, work, education and leisure. The diversity of functions, scale and setting of the components . . . fully illustrate the architectural principles of 'organic architecture.'"

These structures—despite the distance between them—composed one serial nomination to UNESCO. In the octet are four Midwest properties: Taliesin, Spring Green; Jacobs House, Madison (a prototype for Usonian architecture); Unity Temple, Oak Park, Illinois; and Robie House (Prairie style), Chicago. The other four are Taliesin West, Scottsdale, Arizona; Guggenheim Museum, New York City; Fallingwater, Mill Run, Pennsylvania; and Hollyhock House, Los Angeles.

As of 2022, only twenty-four of the 1,154 properties on the World Heritage List were in the United States. Twelve are national or international parks. What else makes the cut? Independence Hall in Philadelphia, the Statue of Liberty in New York City, and San Antonio Missions, for starters.

Taliesin's scenic surroundings—the curvy Wyoming Valley, home of Wright's ancestors—helped inspire him to create an architectural style that was way ahead of its time. He felt no need to mimic fussy, ornate European roots.

Designs were in sync with the natural environment. Construction favored natural, indigenous materials and sleek but simple furnishings. Basic geometric shapes, inside and out, were cleanly and cleverly grouped.

Wright would rotate Taliesin furnishings to give the buildings more life, staff say. Public tours began in the 1990s. Now other experiences are possible, too.

Private retreats for groups, indoors and outdoors, are booked on the 800-acre Taliesin grounds and its buildings. Prices and types of experiences vary. Add farm-to-table meals of multiple courses, summer camps for children, and private tours that address personal interests.

Open spring into fall at **Frank Lloyd Wright Visitor Center** is **Riverview Terrace Café**, whose menu incorporates food grown on-site and at nearby farms. Big windows in the café, a Wright design, show off the Wisconsin River: the architect considered the building his gateway to Taliesin.

IN THE NEIGHBORHOOD

Professional actors at **American Players Theatre** perform, June through November, in two theaters within 110 woodsy acres near Spring Green. Pack a picnic, then hike uphill (or board a quick shuttle) to an outdoor amphitheater where sounds of wildlife sometimes enrich productions, especially as dusk arrives. Downhill is a smaller, indoor theater. In the repertoire of plays presented in rotation are Shakespearean and other classics, plus contemporary works. americanplayers.org, (608) 588-2361

Colorful **Spring Green General Store**, a favored gathering spot, adds flair to in-house bakery and comfort foods in its café. Merchandise is a delight, too: part clothing/accessories boutique, greeting card shop, spice mart, toy store for all ages. Bring a lawn chair to free, outdoor, annual musical tributes to the Beatles (Labor Day) and Bob Dylan (Sunday before Memorial Day). springgreengeneralstore.com, (608) 588-7070

Eight miles southwest is **House on the Rock**, an unusual exercise in architecture that holds the late founder Alex Jordan's stunning mishmash of collections—dollhouses, armor, model ships, crown jewels, robot orchestra, world's largest indoor carousel. Not a work of Wright's. Outside: Asian and sculpture gardens. thehouseontherock.com, (608) 935-3639

Linger throughout the year at **Arcadia Books**, whose coffee bar sells bakery and sandwiches, too. Known for hosting author presentations and book clubs. Posts "wish lists" of titles useful to local schools and nonprofits in need. readinutopia.com, (608) 588-7638

Thousands attend the juried **Spring Green Arts and Craft Fair**, downtown on the first full weekend in June. All 200-some vendors sell original work in categories that include crafts, glass, graphics, handwrought jewelry, paintings, photography, pottery, sculpture, and textiles. For event details and more about the area: springgreen.com, (608) 588-2054.

Closest state park: **Tower Hill**, whose shot tower manufactured lead shot until 1869. See the 180-foot-tall shaft—part wood, part stone—that dropped the shot from smelting house to finishing house. dnr.wisconsin.gov

Stockholm

Population 78

Taste of Sweden

stockholmwisconsin.com

The too-quick darkening of sky near twilight means a storm is approaching, but most of the dozen fishermen don't seem to notice.

A stocky guy with multiple piercings and a deep pink Mohawk is an exception. He totes ashore his catch of the day, a 31-inch northern pike. Not a bad way to end a Tuesday.

The fisherman lives just across the waterway, Lake Pepin. We size up his fish while standing on a pier of rocks in Stockholm—not Sweden's capital but one of the tiniest incorporated communities in Wisconsin.

I don't expect fish this big or fishermen this conspicuous in a village defined by its Swedish flags, freight train traffic, mix of genteel artists and small-town sensibilities. What we have is a mix of surprises.

Most people who visit Stockholm come for the day. They stop to stretch, nibble, and shop while driving the Great River Road. The tiny town flaunts its Swedish heritage, although some with personal or business investments are transplants who respect the past but have no Swedish ancestry.

The rebirth of genuine enthusiasm for local history began in 2006, when eighty-five Swedes initiated a pilgrimage to Wisconsin, to perform

IN THE NEIGHBORHOOD

Lisa Carlson, semifinalist for Best Chef Midwest, does the cooking at **Chef Shack** in Bay City, population 441. Partner Carrie Summer, a pastry specialist, rounds out the fine, compact menu at the cozy restaurant. The duo caught the attention of James Beard Foundation judges after selling mini doughnuts (with cardamom), tacos (beef tongue filling), burgers (bison), and ice cream ("trailer-made organic") from their Twin Cities food truck. Open spring through autumn. chefshackbaycity.com

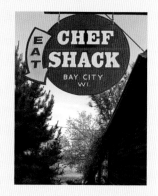

The from-scratch menu covers a big chalkboard and changes often at **Harbor View Café**, Pepin, population 731. Think beef curry with jasmine rice, mushrooms stuffed with cheeses on linguine, red snapper wrapped in smoked salmon and poached. Add homemade bread, an apple cider mimosa. Open from spring into autumn. harborviewpepin.com, (715) 442-3893

Savor fresh pasta and wines from around the world at **Vino in the Valley** in a remote river valley near Maiden Rock, population 115. Pizzas come from a stone oven. Dine and linger outdoors, with views of a vineyard and countryside. Listen to local musicians. Play

cornhole. Open May through September; then business hours shift with the season. vinointhevalley.com, (715) 639-6677

The author of *Little House on the Prairie* was born near Pepin, and artifacts at **Laura Ingalls Wilder Museum** are devoted to pioneer times. Visit the birth site, too. The museum is the starting point for a highway route that links historic Wilder sites throughout the nation. Open May through October. lauraingallspepin.com, (715) 513-6383

Make room for a scoop or two at century-old **Nelson Cheese Factory** in Nelson, population 322, where the line for fresh ice cream during summer is long—as in outside the door—but worth it. Buy cheeses and other Wisconsin products, too. nelsoncheese.com, (715) 673-4725

an emotion-filled play about their Bjurtjarn ancestors who settled the Wisconsin Stockholm.

Locals described it as a powerful story, one that didn't require Swedish roots to appreciate. "When they got here, it was like they were touching sacred ground," one recalled. Stockholm and Bjurtjarn became unofficial sister cities.

Downtown is the **Stockholm Institute**, a local history museum in a former post office. Visit on weekends and notice the photo of Sweden's crown prince, who paid a visit in 1938.

Cardamom is in a spice blend that **Stockholm Pie** uses in Stockholm Apple, topped with a streusel crumble. Lingonberry Lemon is a sweet-tart pie option. From the café come the open-faced Smoked Salmon Smörgås (served on crisp rye flatbread) and the Stockholm, smoked turkey and provolone with lingonberries as well as mayo. stockholmpieand generalstore.com, (715) 442-5505

StockHome creates a world of *hygge*—the Scandinavian term for contentment and comfort—in a boutique for home furnishings and regional art, highlighting heritage in design choices and products. On Facebook, (715) 442-2266

Contemporary Nordic fashions are stocked at **Scandihoo**, whose owners are local artists with Scandinavian roots. Look for Cuckoo Clogs, their own footwear design, in addition to modern and traditional cuckoo clocks. scandihoo.com, (715) 442-4000

Add knitting supplies, wearable art, stylish kitchenware, hand-thrown pottery, and other art at additional shops. The assortment makes Stockholm atypical for its size.

Few also would expect racks of clunky bicycles, each painted a bright Swede blue, at key locations. The community bikes are free to use.

Overnight guests should expect little company, outside of train whistles, after sunset. Wails of the rail—six in two hours, when I chose to count them a while back—seem to define the village as much as the little Swedish flags that flap above flower boxes.

WideSpot, an upstairs performance space, is a long-ago opera house that subsequently was a high school basketball court and roller-skating rink. Traveling musicians find their way here, occasionally from abroad.

As winter nears, *God Jul* festivities on three December weekends observe the Christmas season and winter solstice. *Jultomten*—Father Christmas, in Sweden—arrives. Fire dancers, bonfires, ice candles, and luminaries soften the darkness and chill. Holiday markets, indoors and outside, pop up in and near Stockholm.

Viroqua

Population 4,504

The Driftless Café

driftlesscafe.com
(608) 637-7778

Outside the door is a line of would-be diners. We were smart to make dinner reservations on this summer Thursday night.

The Driftless Café is on the radar of serious foodies, despite the town's out-of-the-way location: 30 bucolic and often-hilly miles from the nearest interstate highway. Count the James Beard Foundation among those who have taken notice: Luke Zahm in 2017 made the cut as semifinalist for Best Chef Midwest. He and his wife, Ruthie, co-own the restaurant.

What an understatement to say that they are passionate about Wisconsin's Driftless Area, where they grew up, and food grown locally. A list of farms and other local products fills two chalkboards at The Driftless.

In Vernon County—home base—are at least 200 certified organic farms, and much of their bounty makes it into the café's menu, which changes nightly and might not be decided upon until that afternoon.

In 2020, Luke was tapped to host *Wisconsin Foodie*, a long-standing and popular public television show about the state's ever-evolving cuisine. He travels statewide to introduce a mix of culinary trendsetters and long-standing foodways.

That means he's not home as much, but his imprint stays strong as others work the Driftless kitchen when he cannot. They are led by Chicago native Mary Kastman as executive chef: she was a Beard award

WORTHY DETOURS

Vernon County has the highest concentration of round barns in Wisconsin. Ten still stand, and most were built between 1890 and 1930; the design was deemed easier to build and more resistant to wind.

Fifteen round barns were built by Alga "Algie" Shivers (1889–1978), a carpenter and son of a slave who used the Underground Railroad to get to Wisconsin. No more than four round barns by Shivers still stand.

Shivers's family farmed near Hillsboro (population 1,397) in the Cheyenne Valley, the state's biggest rural Black settlement in the nineteenth century. The schools, churches, and sports teams of these nearly 150 settlers and their European immigrant neighbors were among the first in Wisconsin to be integrated.

For self-guided driving tours, check out vernoncountyhistory .org, (608) 637-7396.

FAST FACTS

Headquarters for **Organic Valley** is La Farge, population 730, and 15 miles east of Viroqua. No U.S. cooperative owned by organic farmers is bigger. It was organized by seven farmers in 1988, to prevent family farm extinction, and grew to around 1,800 members. organic valley.coop, (888) 444-6455

Thirteen miles southeast is Viola, population 676, and headquarters for **GoMacro**, a mother-daughter business that produces plant-based protein and other nutrition bars with 100 percent renewable energy (wind, solar power). Products earn raves from *Forbes*, *O* (the Oprah magazine). The first recipe was created after a diagnosis of breast cancer. Owners operate a 120-acre farm with veggies and orchards. gomacro .com, (833) 466-2276

FAST FIVE

Driftless Books and Music, in a cavernous tobacco warehouse with hardwood floors and many nooks for browsing and nest-ling, might well be the biggest bookstore in Wisconsin. Owner Eddy Nix categorizes and crams 500,000 books and other media (comics, sheet music, LPs) onto shelves, bins. A beer can collec-tion, in-your-face bumper stick-ers, vintage oddities, and original art (like a smiling critter made with repurposed metals) add character. Lose your way while meandering. Rock and read in the little play area for children. Some nights, musicians entertain on the house piano or with their own instruments. driftlessbooks .com, (608) 638-2665

The largeness of **Viroqua Food Cooperative** demonstrates devotion to organic and locally grown food. It's a community hangout as well as a grocery. Look for produce grown close to home, Wisconsin cheeses that win international awards, small-batch syrups, butcher shop meats, craft beer, and spirits. More attention to dietary restrictions than the average metro market. Try Wisco Pop, based in Viroqua, whose bot-tled organic sodas and seltzers are all about juices, natural sweeteners, spices/herbs. viroquafood.coop, (608) 637-7511; wiscopopsoda.com, (608) 638-7632

A downtown anchor is **Viroqua Public Market**, a car repair garage that morphed into booths for at least one hundred vendors who sell art, jewelry, collectibles, literature, new and recycled clothing, antiques, and flea market items. Also known as Main Street Station. One doorway over is an art cooperative; look for posted bios and artist statements to see who is inspired by the area's natural beauty. viroquapublicmarket .com, (608) 637-1912

Home base for organic roaster **Wonderstate Coffee** is Viroqua. Opera-tions are solar powered. Payments to farmers exceed fair trade prices. Social justice commitments are so deep that the company changed its name from Kickapoo Coffee after 15 years of business. The change was initiated to show greater respect for the Kickapoo Nation. Selling by the cup from Wonderstate's café, in a converted 1940s gas station on Main Street, where bakery might include the buttery French *kouign-amann*. wonderstate.com, (608) 637-2022

Set aside a full Saturday morning, spring into fall, for the outdoor **Viroqua Farmers Market** downtown. Vendors have personality and make time to share slivers of interesting life stories. Soap made with bear fat. Turned wood vases made from downed trees. Handwoven and signed Amish baskets. Keychains forged by Mennonites. A farmer with the patience to explain differences between dozens of types of garlic. Hand-sewn aprons, ugly tomatoes, free AA books—and deliciously predictable garden harvests, too.

For more about the area: viroqua-wisconsin.com, (608) 637-7186.

semifinalist in 2022, so, amazingly two chefs have earned big-time attention in this small town.

Pizza, a menu specialty when I visited this restaurant pre-Zahm, remains popular—based on the number seen paraded from stone oven to table. But the top reason to visit is a taste of fine and offbeat dining with international influences (Arabic during our visit).

A friend and I began with a shared plate of three scallops with slices of grilled squash and a hickory nut *muhammara* (a spicy dip with roasted red peppers, too). Covering the plate was a small glass that, when turned up, released a lingering poof of hickory smoke and smoldered rosemary.

Petite salads came with one of the night's house dressings, a light lemon-peppercorn. Next: the entrees. Maqluba chicken and roasted veggies arrived with turmeric basmati rice and tahini yogurt. A medium-rare beef tenderloin, with kale, sat on a silky mash of potatoes.

For dessert: dark chocolate cake garnished with candied bacon and a drizzle of chocolate over whipped cream.

"We are a 100 percent farmer-funded restaurant," says Ruthie, to drive home the concept of mutual support. "Our farmers believe in what we do" by supporting the restaurant as customers and in other ways for all to live sustainably.

Warrens

Population 544

Warrens Cranberry Festival

cranfest.com
(608) 378-4200

The cranberry is a domestic product, and Wisconsin leads the world in production, harvesting nearly two-thirds of the United States crop in 2022. Nobody is prouder of this than the people of Warrens, whose annual ode to the berry began in 1973 and grew into the globe's largest cranberry event.

Wear good walking shoes to mosey through three miles of vendors. For sale are arts/crafts, antiques, flea market finds, farmers market products. Some people bring a collapsible cart on wheels and fill it with most anything imaginable: garden art, quilts, cookware, rugs, sports-themed apparel, lotions, hunting/fishing gear, unusual gifts.

FAST FACTS

Wisconsin State Cranberry Growers Association strongly prefers the word "marsh" to "bog" when referring to areas where cranberries are grown.

Ninety-five percent of the state's crop is used to produce cranberry sauce or juice. Only 3 percent is sold as fresh fruit.

QUICK DETOURS

Follow the **Cranberry Highway**, a 50-mile self-guided drive, in late September to late October and see bright red cranberry beds in addition to brilliant fall leaf colors. The route begins 25 miles northeast of Warrens. Download a map at visitwisrapids.com/cranberry-highway.

Thirty-five miles northeast of Warrens is Pittsville, population 813; at the high school is the nation's only cranberry science class. Students in early autumn lead 2-hour **Splash of Red Cranberry Tours** that explain the business and process of growing the fruit. Tours end at the high school, where students make and serve a cranberry-themed lunch. Proceeds from ticket sales provide scholarships to Future Farmers of America members. (715) 884-6412

These 1,300 vendors come to Warrens from up to twenty-five states for the three-day festival.

Among the eighty-some food booths are culinary experiments that make the berry the star. Concoctions such as coconut shrimp with cranberry sauce, cranberry chicken alfredo pizza, cranberry mac and cheese, chocolate cranberry cookie dough on a stick.

How popular is the cranberry jubilee, served over vanilla ice cream? The topping is made in a giant skillet, 4.5 feet in diameter, and served 6 hours per day. Cream puffs, scones, cookies, cheesecakes, smoothies, shakes, wines, and lattes contain cranberries, too.

Two-pound bags of fresh cranberries are a good, discounted buy. Free for sampling are new or hard-to-find cranberry products, such as juice blends and dried berry varieties. Volunteers for nonprofits—be it the Lions Club or a high school football team—raise money by parking cars, distributing samples, running errands, providing security.

Gone is the annual cranberry recipe contest, an amazing and sometimes odd spectacle of entries in all courses that I helped judge years ago. Our big winner in the processed cranberry category was lasagna with dried berries mixed into the ricotta layer and the sauce. Much tastier than it probably sounds.

When I returned to Warrens a decade later, festival cofounder June Potter and a golf cart guided me through the ever-expanding grounds and deep sea of shoppers. We made sure to see her great-granddaughter's winning entry in the contest for largest cranberry: her Beaver Creek Sundance berry weighed in at 5.47 grams.

June's great-grandchildren, if they choose to be cranberry growers, will be the family's eighth generation to do so. The matriarch described Warrens as a poor village in the 1970s: "We wanted to improve the area and wondered what we could promote."

A $500 profit from Warrens' centennial celebration was turned into a bet on cranberries. One with a big payoff.

The first festival began with a dance at the town hall and midnight coronation of royalty. Dancing moved to the volunteer fire station the next night, after firemen played baseball during the day. Turtle and frog races—"bring your own or we'll have 'em available"—got cut along the way, but opportunities for cranberry marsh and harvest tours grew.

Today it's an all-in effort for the rural area. Tomah School District students have Friday off during the festival, and teachers get an in-service day. Festival profits have helped pay for playground equipment, school trips to Washington, D.C., a bigger truck for the volunteer fire department.

June says local residents who charge a few bucks for festival parking "might make enough to pay their property taxes by the time the festival ends." A friend, now departed, years ago told June that "we created a monster—but it's a good one" because the event makes money, connects the residents, and puts Warrens on the map.

The festival marks the start of the annual cranberry harvest, but **Cranberry Discovery Center** in Warrens is home to all things cranberry throughout the year. Downstairs is a museum; upstairs is cranberry-centric merchandise and a café—all in a renovated berry warehouse. discovercranberries.com, (608) 378-4878

Westby

Population 2,332

Dregne's Scandinavian Gifts

dregnesscandinavian.gift
(608) 634-4414

A meaningful relationship doesn't happen by accident. It requires work and is long-standing in Westby, which unabashedly flaunts its Norwegian heritage. That is especially evident at Dregne's, a shop with hard-to-find imports—especially Norwegian products—and finely crafted items made in the United States.

Solje jewelry, *lefse* grills, leather-wood clogs, collectible trolls and gnomes are in stock. So are increasingly rare Arne Hasle *nisse* dolls, and an array of Christmas decor stays up all year.

Jana Dregne, co-owner with her husband, Dave, since 1975 has championed her community's mission

to stay true to its roots. She knows and promotes what makes Westby authentically Norwegian, beyond the rosemaled benches on Main Street, nisse cutouts on buildings, and a giant Norseman statue near outskirts of town.

The area was settled by Norwegian immigrants in 1848. Murals, signage, carvings, and *stabbur* (storehouse) design for tourist info symbolize a deep respect for the motherland's foods, crafts, and culture. Especially during **Syttende Mai**, the May celebration of Norwegian independence, revived in Westby in 1969.

Sons of Norway presents a breakfast of smoked salmon, herring, "five of heart" waffles (a reference to design) with lingonberries and

FAST FACT

Skiers from around the world come to Westby for winter ski jumping championships on hills four miles north of town. **Snowflake Ski Jump Tournaments** began in 1923, and modern-day competitors are airborne more than 100 yards after speeding down the Olympic-sized jump in excess of 50 miles per hour. Shorter jumps on smaller hills are training grounds for ski jumping. snowflakeskiclub.com, (608) 634-3211

QUICK DETOUR

Twelve hilly, curvy miles north-west of Westby is **Norskedalen Heritage Center**, which preserves nature, culture, and rural architec-ture. Within 400 acres is Bekkum Homestead (a dozen unusual Nor-wegian farm structures); nearby is Thrunegaarden (a furnished, one-room school, 1853 log home, and other restored buildings). Miles of hiking trails and occasional classes in folk arts, Norwegian traditions. norskedalen.org, (608) 452-3424

more. A traditional meatball and lefse dinner sells out at two Lutheran churches that are one block apart.

Pølse, Norway's version of a hot dog/sausage, is wrapped in lefse and served at an outdoor stand. Gallons of *rømmegrøt*, a rich pudding, are savored by the individual portion and gobbled at an eating contest.

Hardanger embroidery, rosemaling, wood carving, lefse making, and fiddle making are demonstrated in an area devoted to heritage. For raffling: something larger, such as a rosemaled trunk or *kubbestol* (chair intricately carved from a log).

Visitors learn the difference between rosemaling styles. A gathering for fans of old-time music is open to whoever wants to listen or show up with an instrument, be it accordion or fiddle. westbysyttendemai.com

At other times of year, Jana eats lingonberries with yogurt or *sand-bakkels*, a light sugar cookie. "More antioxidants than blueberries," she says, emphasizing that she's not alone. Sons of Norway has ninety members. At least one dozen are in the Westby rosemaling club.

The annual summer Carve In at the Bekkum (the public library) draws amateur and pro woodcarvers to learn from an award-winning craftsperson. The 1892 Thoreson House, a museum, is a repository for artifacts and genealogy records. westbywihistory.com

It all adds up to the Norske-rich reputation that Westby has earned and apparently has spread internationally.

When travelers from Norway visit, and Jana says some come by the busload to find Westby, she repeatedly hears, "You're more Norwegian than we are—look at your carvers, your rosemalers."

FAST FOUR

Eat lefse with house-made meatballs and mashed potatoes, or as a wrap with scrambled eggs at **Borgen's Café**, where mini gnomes hold salt and pepper shakers. The Feisty Norwegian sandwich is grilled chicken with Cajun seasoning. Save room for pie; sour cream and raisin is a specialty. borgenscafe.com, (608) 634-4003

Almost anything goes in the three-floor **Treasures on Main**, where one hundred-some consigners sell a hodgepodge of antiques, furniture, books, art, and artisan products. Confirmation of Norwegian culture is easy to find. treasuresonmain.net, (608) 634-4474

One block off the main drag downtown is **Westby House Inn**, which mixes history and contemporary comforts in five guest rooms. Breakfast, served on china, comes with gourmet flair. One possibility: cherry sundae French toast. westbyhouse.com, (608) 634-4112

Milk from small family farms turns into award-winning cottage cheese, French onion dip, and other dairy products at **Westby Creamery**, in business since 1903. Stock up at the creamery's store downtown, where fresh cheese curds are sold twice a week. westbycreamery.com, (608) 634-3181

For more about the area: westbychamber.com, (608) 634-4011.

FAN FAVORITE

Sixty miles north of Westby is Blair, population 1,325, whose **Country-side Lefse** since 1965 has made the product with "real" potatoes—not instant—and dough is flattened by hand with rolling pins—not machinery. The lefse is sold to grocery stores, restaurants, and organizations whose members lack the time and patience to make lefse on their own for *lutefisk* or other types of Norwegian dinners. lefse.com, (608) 989-2363

She is told that the practicing of traditional crafts has faded abroad and feels confident that won't happen in her town. Parents teach Norwegian traditions to the next generation, Jana says, in hopes that the heritage is preserved.

"You have to get to a certain age to appreciate your heritage," Jana acknowledges, but she also believes the Norse visitors who declare, "When you go the United States, you have to go to Westby."

Wisconsin Dells

Population 2,942

H. H. Bennett Studio and Museum

hhbennettstudio.wisconsinhistory.org
(608) 253-3523

We can thank or blame Henry Hamilton Bennett for his work to make Wisconsin Dells a major vacation destination. His landscape photography is what alerted early-time tourists to an area best known, until the mid-1800s, as a rough-and-tumble logging port and railroad stop.

Today the area is a top Midwest tourist stop that has more than 8,000 hotel rooms and nearly one hundred major attractions. The area's natural beauty no longer is the only lure.

The Wisconsin River weaves through this hospitality-driven and thrill-a-minute community. Near downtown are sandstone cliffs and canyons with unusual rock formations and deep gorges. One of Bennett's most famous photos is titled *Leaping the Chasm*, a freeze-frame of his son jumping between a cliff ledge and Stand Rock.

The photographer's 1875 workplace, a state historic site, is among the nation's oldest continually operated photo studios. The best souvenir for visiting is a tintype photo of yourself, produced with the same technology of Bennett's era.

NATURAL CHARMERS

The natural world is the star at these destinations south of Wisconsin Dells.

Five miles: Cliffs and woods surround the water at **Mirror Lake State Park**, where a much-loved supper club operates from spring into autumn. **Ishnala**—"by itself alone" in Winnebago language—is a former ceremonial ground that turned into a trading post; original architecture remains. Reservations not accepted; prepare to make this your destination for the night. dnr.wisconsin.gov, (608) 254-2333; ishnala.com, (608) 253-1771

Eight miles: The 300-acre **International Crane Foundation** is the only place where all fifteen species of the bird live. Researchers work with specialists on five continents to secure the cranes' future survival. Tour the campus, open May through October. savingcranes.org, (608) 356-9462

Ten miles: **Aldo Leopold Shack and Farm**, a National Historic Landmark, marks the spot where the conservation pioneer and *A Sand County Almanac* author learned how to restore the health of neglected land. Down the road are hiking trails and the environmentally sustainable **Aldo Leopold Legacy Center**, which has a visitor center. aldoleopold.org, (608) 355-0279

Fifteen miles: Hike the quartzite bluffs at **Devil's Lake**, the largest state park in Wisconsin, with almost 30 miles of trails and a 360-acre lake. Rock climbing is not prohibited or promoted: it is done at your own risk; permits are not issued. dnr.wisconsin.gov, (608) 356-8301

Twenty-five miles: Even on hot summer days, **Parfrey's Glen** feels cool. Wisconsin's first State Natural Area is a moss-covered glen with a waterfall and deep gorge with a cold stream running through it in the Baraboo Hills. dnr.wisconsin.gov

"He enthusiastically partnered with the railroad company and arranged for some of his stereo-view images—and printed information about the wonders of the area—to be placed in passenger cars," says David Rambow, historic site director. Sets of photos were donated to public libraries "to promote his work and encourage interest in the vicinity as a wonderful and safe place for a middle-class vacation."

Bennett was a carpenter who turned to photography because of a Civil War injury to his hand. Landscape photos made him well known, as did images of other Midwest places that he was contracted to photograph, but neither paid for most of his family's bills.

"Although studio portraiture was his 'bread and butter' source of income, Henry Bennett disliked doing them," David says. The photographer delegated the work to his assistants and his wife, Frankie, who died prematurely of respiratory issues at age 36.

"Henry seems to have blamed himself, as he had her working around all the photo chemicals" in the darkroom. She also "encouraged him in all his struggles up to the time of her death," and that includes helping him through recurrent bouts of depression. He was a humble man who worried about financial security.

FAST FIVE

Wisconsin Dells is known as Waterpark Capital of the World because of the high concentration. **Noah's Ark** is the nation's largest waterpark at 70 acres; it has 3 miles of waterslides. At **Wilderness Resort** is the country's biggest indoor-outdoor waterpark, equivalent to twelve football fields. noahsarkwaterpark.com, (608) 254-6351; wildernessresort .com, (608) 253-9729

For the spa lover: Water is a prime feature at 26-acre **Sundara**, for adults only. Outdoors is a heated infinity pool, for soaking in all seasons. Indoors is a bathhouse with five-step purifying bath ritual. sundaraspa .com, (888) 735-8181

On-water excursions are a popular way to explore Wisconsin Dells. The **Original Wisconsin Ducks** are amphibious vehicles whose passengers travel on water and land. In business since 1946; tours last 1 hour. wisconsinducktours.com, (608) 254-8751

Dells Boat Tours cruise the Upper and Lower Dells, with shore landings and the option to add dinner at sunset. Or take a ghost tour that begins with an up-river ride at dark. Tour length varies. Late May through October. dellsboats.com, (608) 254-8555

For more about the area: wisdells.com, (800) 223-3557.

What was known as Kilbourn City was renamed Wisconsin Dells in 1931, and the community is a part of four counties—Sauk, Juneau, Columbia, and Adams—today. On the outskirts is **Ho-Chunk Casino, Hotel and Convention Center**, a minimal presence for the tribal nation that was forced out of Wisconsin by the federal government in the 1830s. Those who returned at the turn of the century would supplement income as seasonal farm laborers by selling handicrafts and performing for tourists.

The later works of Bennett, who considered the Ho-Chunk his friends, included portraits and other photos of the tribal nation.

Wonewoc

Population 758

Wonewoc Spiritualist Camp

campwonewoc.org
(608) 464-7770

A mural next to the public library welcomes Highway 33 passersby to Wonewoc, and the artwork's bright colors make it easy to miss a little sign for what brings us here.

We take a right and head uphill two blocks, park, and start meandering. At bluff's edge, we see the stately 1911 St. Paul's Lutheran downtown, but the spirit moves people with a different type of faith—or hope—to the ground where we stand.

Since 1874, spiritualists have come here to commune, appreciate nature, and communicate with the dead. Now known as Wonewoc Spiritual Camp, the 30 mostly wooded acres are a magnet for the confused, curious, and crestfallen who seek guidance, comfort, healing, introspection.

I need not have felt self-conscious about showing up without notice. That happens often, says the Rev. Carol Luetkens, director. Visitors are welcome to roam the grounds, early June to early September, but there's no guarantee you'll get time with a medium without an appointment. They are scheduled on the hour and half hour, $62 for 30 minutes in 2022.

On a chalkboard near the camp entrance are the first names of mediums at work; they come to Wonewoc to spend all or a part of summer, staying in simply furnished camp cottages that double as their office.

The tiny cottages are similar in design but unique in appearance. One has flowers growing in a box and basket, plus a small American flag. A neighbor has a door painted blue, silhouette cutouts of wildlife, and "Spirit Lodge" sign. Next comes a two-tone teal cabin with matching bench and golden whirligigs.

Outside each little building is a different number, and that's how customers know where to go for their time with a psychic medium. Mark, from the area, is painting his cabin but stops to chat amicably. Between appointments, he cares for this temporary home like he owns it.

Inside a cabin are two cushioned chairs separated by a small, cloth-covered table. Nearby are incense sticks, a sage smudge stick, small dish with smooth and colorful stones. Against a wall painted light green is a twin-size bed, next to a chest of drawers. Bedspread and throw rug are a pleasant mismatch of stripes.

For overnight guests: clean, motel-like accommodations that are sparsely furnished. The camp plan is to add a school for spiritualists, eventually.

Too skittish or frugal to book time here? Too wary of where a reading might lead? A smaller first step is an online church service, held at midweek throughout the year.

The National Spiritualist Association of Churches does not believe their religion conflicts with Christianity, and much of what I heard online seemed benign enough: Meditative breathing to flush away worries and negativity. Advice to nourish yourself by loving yourself. Prayers for those who are alone. Reminders that we all contribute to the energy of the universe.

And, afterward, brief "spirit meetings" in which a spiritualist shares blips of what she sees: Your grandma, who's knitting and praying. Your dad in a doorway—he likes being with you. A man on your mother's side—he's a stinker, trying to splash you and wants you to take that dive.

"And I'll leave that with love and blessings," the medium says, as these messages end. What you hear is up to you to decipher, run with, or leave behind.

DECENT DETOURS

Wonewoc is on the 22-mile **400 State Trail**, named after a passenger train that traveled 400 miles in 400 minutes between Chicago and Minneapolis. The bike route, on a former railroad bed, hooks up to the 32.5-mile **Elroy–Sparta State Trail**, the nation's first rail-to-trail project. dnr.wisconsin.gov

Nine miles west is Hillsboro, population 1,397, and proud of its Czech heritage. The three-day **Cesky Den** in June involves a polka Mass and plenty of roast pork, sauerkraut, dumplings at Firemen's Park. hillsborowi.com, (608) 489-3446

Within 25 miles northwest of Wonewoc are additional diversions:

Ontario, population 534, is a popular **Kickapoo River** access point. Outfitters rent canoes, kayaks, and inner tubes to navigate the highly crooked river (it's fewer than 70 miles between end points, but the river flows 125 miles). ontariowi.com, (608) 337-4381

Take a steam train ride at nonprofit **Mid-Continent Railway Museum**, which since 1963 has protected and restored the equipment and attitude of the Golden Age of Railroads, when most small towns had a train station that connected them to the wider world. Near North Freedom, population 603. midcontinent.org, (608) 522-4261

For breakfast, lunch, or pie: **Dorset Valley Schoolhouse Restaurant**, where a slice might mean chocolate hickory nut or lemon sour cream. A chalkboard lists daily specials in this restored one-room schoolhouse from 1848, near Wilton, population 532. Dine on Amish-made chairs and tables, buy raw honey by the quart, and look for Amish farms along nearby Highway 131. On Facebook, (608) 343-5889

For more about the area: driftlesswisconsin.com, (608) 326-6658.

Southeast

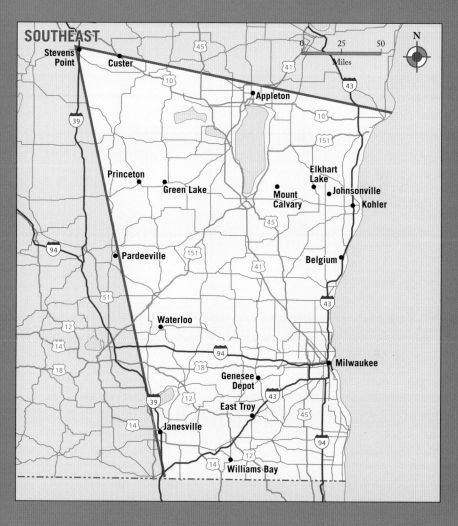

Discover a hodgepodge of delightful diversions, made by people and nature.

Circle Lake Winnebago—our largest inland lake—by car and pay particular attention to the less-populated eastern side, where farms sell cheeses, veggies, and other organic fare. Detour into Wisconsin's rural Holyland, hamlets that may have little more than a Catholic church.

By foot, follow the Ice Age National Scenic Trail to 60-foot Parnell Tower in Sheboygan County, to see for miles above treetops. The view is the Northern Unit of Kettle Moraine State Forest, 30,000 acres of hills, vales, and prairieland formed by glacier movement. Ice Age Visitor Center, in Fond du Lac County, explains the difference between a kettle, moraine, and more.

Trails here and in the forest's 22,000-acre Southern Unit are big with mountain bikers, hikers, and cross-country skiers. Signage marks the 115-mile Kettle Moraine Scenic Drive, which leads to additional treats: historic sites, artsy farms, religious shrines, Old World dining, rural roadhouses.

The Niagara Escarpment—thick, limestone cliffs that are ancient geological formations—weaves through six Wisconsin counties, then dips underwater in Lake Michigan. The 650-mile ridge also is what makes the thunder of Niagara Falls so dramatic.

Belgium

Population 2,421

Luxembourg American Cultural Society

lacs.lu
(920) 476-5086

It's one thing to know your ancestral roots and be proud. Quite another to have the motherland's heads of state take notice, visit, and support you. Repeatedly.

That's what happened when this facility—a museum, genealogy center, and hub for cultural programming/support—opened in 2009. His Royal Highness the Grand Duke Henri of Luxembourg showed up for the dedication. The European nation's prime minister visited three years later.

Other international dignitaries visit, too, and that was years before Tom Barrett—longtime Milwaukee mayor—was appointed

U.S. ambassador to Luxembourg. It certainly didn't hurt him to have this respected international society 40 miles from home.

The cultural institute in this village is the only one trusted by Luxembourg leadership to assist with dual-citizenship requests; the center helped about 3,000 families by 2022. The research center is the largest for Luxembourg studies and genealogy outside of Luxembourg (in archives are 6,000 surname files). The society typically arranges multiple trips to the homeland annually.

"It's so easy to get immersed in the culture here," says Tara Williams, who heads Belgium's chamber of commerce. "The culture is a unique identifier for us."

Inside an 1872 Luxembourgian stone barn—dismantled, moved 10 miles, and reassembled in Belgium—is Roots and Leaves Museum. One-half delves into Luxembourger immigration to Wisconsin in the 1840s. Most were farmers with hopes of starting a better life.

"The Great Famine of those times was not limited to potatoes and Ireland," notes curator Serena Stuettgen. The Midwest was a frontier, the land was theirs to work, and the area resembled their native country.

The museum's other half tells the story of Luxembourg, a country comparable to Rhode Island in size and the world's only grand duchy. The push-pull of changing boundaries and country ownership ended with Luxembourg's independence in 1815.

A grand duke or duchess rules the constitutional monarchy; the country also has a prime minister and democratic parliament. At its borders are Germany, Belgium, and France.

The Wisconsin museum's furnishings, artwork, exhibit panels, and display cases were crafted by artisans in Luxembourg. All were gifts from the country. The same goes for the entrance's almost 15-foot-tall showpiece: a steel sculpture of a tree, with photos of modern-day and ancestral families as the leaves and—under glass among the roots— twelve stones that represent each of the nation's cantons (states).

The cultural society's 3,000-some members represent several countries. The board of directors is international, too, and includes Luxembourg's ambassador to the United States. When the village marked its centennial in 2022, the celebration generated international well wishes.

"People haven't really strayed too far in one hundred years," Tara says of her area's residents, and language classes are offered so the native tongue is not lost.

Locals tend to speak Luxembourgish as though it were the 1800s, because that's how one generation passed it to the next in Wisconsin. Tara says the antiquated phrases fascinate modern-day visitors from Luxembourg.

Then there's the fun stuff, like Luxembourg Fest Week in August. One family surname is honored each year, which turns the event into an international family reunion. Festival royalty are crowned after a Sunday morning polka Mass.

Luxembourg bands typically travel to Wisconsin to perform. Leading the parade is a traditional *Hammelsmarsch* of sheep and their herders; the same happens at festivals in Luxembourg. To drink: Bofferding beer,

MORE PRIDE OF HERITAGE

Six miles north of Belgium is Cedar Grove, population 2,101, which throws its heart into **Holland Festival** in July. The 2022 gathering was the seventy-fifth, which makes it twice as old as Belgium's Luxembourg Fest.

Street scrubbers with wide brooms wash Van Altena Avenue to open the Dutch festival, and then comes racing while wearing wooden shoes (bring your own or rent them). Expect lots of dancing in clogs, too: in Cedar Grove, children begin to learn traditional, synchronized Dutch dances at age 4.

What else? Buy a pair of shoes hand-carved by the local *klompenmaker.* For sale is glazed Delft pottery and other items from the Netherlands. To eat: *oliebollen* (doughnut holes), *worstenbroodjes* (sausage rolls), and conventional festival foods.

Two museums—**TeRonde House** and **Het Museum**—preserve local history, including Dutch artifacts. holland-festival.com, cedargrovewi.com/museums, (920) 668-6295

Ramborn hard cider, Domaines Vinsmoselle wines, and other Luxembourgian imports.

Most unusual is the eating of *treipen*—a sausage with equal parts meat, veggies, and pig blood. It is Luxembourg's version of black pudding, but Wisconsin butchers tend to use more meat and cabbage than the traditional recipe.

The festival goes through at least 200 pounds of treipen in two days. Some is part of a meal with fried potatoes, applesauce, and slice of rye bread. Some is sold by the frozen pound, for eating later (it's customarily baked or fried).

Thirty-five pounds are set aside for the treipen-eating contest, where the winner usually gobbles about one pound in one minute. The reward? A year of bragging rights, a trophy, and more treipen to take home.

"There are other pockets of Luxembourgers nationally, but ours might be the largest and longest-running festival," Tara says. "People who are Luxembourgers here love it and are proud to love it."

Custer

Population not tracked

Midwest Renewable Energy Fair

theenergyfair.org
(715) 592-6595

Deeply rooted in central Wisconsin is a passion to protect the environment. The University of Wisconsin–Stevens Point, 7 miles west of Custer,
set up the nation's first major in conservation education in 1946.

Why there? Within a 20-mile radius of the university's College of
Natural Resources are 160,000 acres of forest and 32,000 acres of wetlands. Also within those parameters is the nonprofit Midwest Renewable
Energy Association, whose staff are devoted to spreading the good
word about ecological stewardship and sustainability.

The MREA's annual summer Energy Fair is the nation's largest
and longest-running grassroots event of its kind. It began in 1990 as
a response to the first Gulf War and average consumer's dependence
on fossil fuels. Concerned families gathered in a farm kitchen to hash
out what and how they could teach others to consider clean energy
technologies.

IN THE NEIGHBORHOOD

Eight miles southeast of Custer is Amherst, population 1,117, whose motto is "small town atmosphere with big city possibilities." The village describes itself as solar friendly and encourages the use of "alternative energy systems and technology."

Look for colorful murals and progressive businesses. Ongoing is restoration of a 1902 opera house. Touring entertainers and topical discussions land at **Jensen Community Center**. jensencenter.org, (715) 824-5202

Central Waters Brewing Company serves Ouisconsing Red Ale and its other beers at an indoor-outdoor taproom. **The Village Hive**, a bakery that also sells local food products, thinks creatively—as in vegan date/fig bars, strawberry/chocolate chip cookies, pear/walnut cream scones. centralwaters.com, (715) 824-2739; thevillagehivebakeryandlocalfoods collective.com, (715) 824-3006

Seven miles south of Amherst is **Artha Sustainable Living Center**, which operates a solar-powered bed-and-breakfast on 23 acres of organic gardens, forest, and fields. arthaonline.com, (715) 824-3463

Closest state park: **Hartman Creek**, on the Chain O' Lakes, has a 7.5-mile trail for horseback riding. In the 1864 Hellestad House, a log cabin, is a nature center. dnr.wisconsin.gov, (715) 258-2372

"The goal was to end the justification for endless wars for oil," says Nick Hylla, MREA executive director. Workshops, demos, and calls to action—at a nearby fairgrounds—brought 3,000 to the area's rolling hills. Efforts were repeated and expanded the next year, and the next, until the fledgling MREA grew to concentrate on energy issues all year.

By 1999, the MREA had a permanent headquarters in Custer, the ReNew the Earth Institute. Ten years later, a second office opened in Milwaukee. The Custer campus is "net zero" because energy comes from sources other than fossil fuels (primarily solar power). midwestrenew.org, (715) 592-6595

The three-day Energy Fair has matured to mix fun with education. Expect musicians, food vendors, kid-friendly events, industry and artisan-product exhibits, and 200-some workshops about sustainability. The event's Clean Energy Career Fair meshes prospective employers and workers. The Clean Transportation Show introduces the latest in electric vehicles, fast charges, and MREA's solar carport.

"There is no shortage of groups talking about how things should be, what should be done, what's wrong and what could be better," Nick acknowledges. "There is, however, a shortage of people dedicated to putting ideas into practice."

He says that's where the MREA excels: the association is a national leader in solar energy instruction. Staff annually provide accredited training for 500-plus people (mainly solar installation professionals, electrical inspectors, teachers). Staff also help homes, schools, businesses, and jurisdictions go solar.

Also on the campus is a new energy storage demonstration lab and education courses—some virtual—for consumers (examples: intro to wind energy systems, energy storage fundamentals, working with electricity).

The first step, for average households, is to see what the summer gathering is all about. The Energy Fair "meets people wherever they may be in their sustainability journey," says Celia Sweet, MREA events manager. "Whether you've attended every fair since 1990, are an industry professional, or have never even considered clean energy and sustainability in your life, you will find something to educate you and inspire action."

East Troy

Population 4,687

Alpine Valley Music Theatre

alpinevalleymusictheatre.org
(262) 642-4400

Music historians have long known Alpine Valley, 4 miles south of East Troy, as a place of significant birth and death.

Blues guitarist Stevie Ray Vaughan and three others died in a helicopter that crashed into an Alpine Valley ski hill in 1990. Around a pole, near the crash site, a bronze band acknowledges the fateful, foggy night.

FAST FACT

Alpine Valley Resort, which no longer owns the outdoor performance space, is best known for downhill skiing, snowboarding, mountain biking, and 27 holes of golfing. At the base of 100 skiable acres is a 120-room hotel. alpinevalleyresort.com, (262) 642-7374

The 35-year-old musician was the opener for Eric Clapton at Alpine Valley Music Theatre and would be inducted posthumously into the Rock and Roll Hall of Fame 25 years later.

Their rural Wisconsin stop was significant for the era's other top recording artists, too. Why? The outdoor music venue's amphitheater was the nation's largest for 16 years (until surpassed by a California project in 1993). Surroundings were pastoral, amid rolling slopes and cornfields.

Rolling Stone would rate Alpine Valley as one of the ten best amphitheaters in America. Among headliners for the opening season's thirty-six shows: Frank Sinatra, Jimmy Buffett, Bob Seger, Helen Reddy, Harry Chapin, Neil Sedaka, and Boz Scaggs.

Lineup and location were a magnetic pull for Generation Jones, including college friends and me, who were eager to check out the setting and sounds of rocker band Chicago in 1977. We subsequently learned to obey the speed limit when near concert grounds to avoid consequences of a speed trap set up in the vicinity on music dates.

Having an actual seat near the stage was a true privilege back then. We were totally content to simply spread a blanket and take turns roaming the hillside grounds and talking to strangers, some foreigners from Illinois, while drinking a beer and watching the sunset.

The venue became best known for Grateful Dead concerts, whose "Dead Head" fans temporarily moved in by the thousands, setting up camp and carrying on, much to the dismay of the area's residents. The rockers would jam on four consecutive dates at a time, until the group was banned after a third show in 1989.

IN THE NEIGHBORHOOD

On a fifth-generation farm, 15 miles west of Alpine Valley, is **Duesterbeck's Brewing Company** in a renovated red barn. Nurture a pint of Crop Duster (a cream ale) or Nutty Bill's Peanut Butter Porter in the microbrewery's taproom or a roomy outdoor patio, where live music is booked. The brewmaster, a co-owner, holds degrees in bacteriology and dentistry. dbcbrewery.com, (262) 729-9771

Three miles north of Alpine Valley is **Grassway Organics**, a family dairy farm with steers, hogs, and poultry, too. An on-farm store sells farm products and natural foods. Pizza nights, May through September, use locally sourced ingredients. grasswayorganics.com, (920) 894-4201

Thirteen miles north is **Old World Wisconsin**, whose restored historic structures create a sense of life in the 1850s on 600 acres near Eagle, population 2,071. Costumed staff at the state historic site demonstrate the work and joys of simpler times. oldworldwisconsin .wisconsinhistory.org, (262) 594-6301

J. Lauber's, an old-time ice cream parlor with oodles of artifacts from the 1930s in East Troy, serves phosphates, malts, floats, and ice-cream treats. The Tortoise, a super-sized turtle sundae, starts with seven scoops of vanilla. Open May through October. (262) 642-3679

Across the street is **East Troy Electric Railroad**, one part museum and one part roundtrip rides to **The Elegant Farmer**, a bakery-deli-market known nationally for apple pie baked in a paper bag. The 10-mile trips on a historic trolley are April through October. Dinner, brunch, and family picnic trains are occasional. easttroyrr.com, (262) 642-3263; elegantfarmer.com, (262) 363-6770

"From people bathing in the pond off of Pond Road, to the music and dancing into the early hours of the morning, Alpine's parking lot was a community in itself," notes alpinestaff.com. Grateful Dead performed twenty times between 1980 and 1989 at Alpine Valley; subsets under other names later performed occasionally.

Alpine Valley grounds and ownership have changed since those carefree days, but the wood roof performance pavilion in the valley remains. "The roof's natural material allows sound to resonate against the hills and valley beautifully, something that theaters with steel structures cannot relate to," explains Ticketmaster's blog.

Seasonal shows continue at the 37,000-capacity site, with the Dave Matthews Band and Jimmy Buffett's Coral Reefers as perennial favorites who are booked for more than one date.

Elkhart Lake

Population 941

Road America

roadamerica.com
(920) 892-4576

The 4.048-mile loop that is Road America ranks among the world's fastest permanent tracks for road racing. My flashbacks of the curvy, glacier-chiseled area are numerous, deep, and personal.

During childhood, the constant buzz of motorsport engines was easy to hear at our farm, 5 miles from the speed of competition. As a teen waitress, tips occasionally would be pit passes—access into the racetrack's inner sanctuary.

We restless summer resort staffers would be motivated, year after year, by unfounded rumors that actor-racer Paul Newman booked a stay. At least two friends met their future husbands during a race weekend; myriad other summer loves were sparked at the track or corner bar in the village.

Much in my life changed after those easygoing years. The family farm morphed into a public hunting ground, for pheasants in particular. The resort where I worked changed names and ownership more than once. The corner bar was replaced by a dining room with white linens and candles.

What stays the same? Road America, in many ways. The facility's 640 acres—hills and ravines near Kettle Moraine State Forest—continue as a car racer's dream. Annual June Sprints (since 1956) remain the Sports Car Club of America's (SCCA) oldest event for amateur road racers.

A local highway engineer turned farmland into the fourteen-turn track by 1955. Before that, car racers competed on public roads—routes of 3.3 and 6.5 miles—until banned by legislation.

The old-time road courses were "a challenging combination of vertical and horizontal curves, and a straightaway for speed," writes Elkhart Lake Historic Race Circuits. The longest races were a series of laps that exceeded 200 miles. Winners of shorter races averaged nearly 90 mph. historicracecircuits.com

Fourteen markers identify and explain these rural routes, which are on the National Register for Historic Places. "The three races held during the period of significance, 1950–1952, quickly established Elkhart Lake as a road racing area rivaling Watkins Glen, New York," drawing nationally known drivers and "tens of thousands of spectators," states the nomination for National Register status. "Character and corridor of the racing route is largely intact."

Road America's original course remains intact, too, making it highly unusual in the racing world. The track has hosted vintage car racing and 500-mile endurance tests, motorcycle and Indy Car competitions. It landed the NASCAR Cup Series in 2021, after a 65-year hiatus for such racing.

RESORTS, RESORTERS

Lakeside getaways are so much a part of Elkhart Lake's history and identity that its high school athletic teams are known as the Resorters. Three resorts remain: the historic Siebkens, mega Osthoff, and boutique Shore Club Wisconsin.

I knew the **Shore Club** as Schwartz Hotel long ago, and it subsequently was renamed Barefoot Bay, then Victorian Village. Locals for decades have favored the property's laid-back Tiki Bar for fine lake views and free live music. choicehotels.com, (920) 876-3323

The Osthoff began as a hotel and morphed into a theater camp for youth before structures were razed and a condo resort of 245 units constructed. On-site are spa services, restaurants, cocktail areas, and conference facilities. osthoff.com, (920) 876-5843

For rent at century-old **Siebkens**, a state historic site, are a mix of condos and historic hotel rooms (Paul Newman stayed while filming the 1969 movie *Winning*). Next to the main dining room—which feels like one big, screened porch in summer—is the Hard Left Lounge, an intimate and almost-hidden cocktail bar. Racing decals and bumper stickers fill walls at Stop-Inn Tavern. siebkens.com, (920) 876-2600

Pontoon rides and watercraft rentals are abundant in Elkhart. Visiting for just the day? Admission is nominal at **Fireman's Park**, where the beach is sandy, and there's ample space to picnic or sunbathe; the volunteer fire department owns the nicely managed park. elkhart lakewi.gov, (920) 876-2122

Look for Amish-made fare, homespun handicrafts, and local produce at the seasonal farmers market at the railroad depot (now a history museum) downtown on Saturday. For more reasons to visit: elkhartlake.com, (920) 876-2385

IN THE NEIGHBORHOOD

Pack a mountain bike, ride a horse, or strap on cross-country skis to get acquainted with the **Kettle Moraine State Forest Northern Unit**, whose pathways include a segment of the Ice Age National Scenic Trail. Especially in autumn, follow the 115-mile **Kettle Moraine Scenic Drive** between Elkhart Lake and Whitewater Lake for a good look at both Northern and Southern units in six counties. dnr.wisconsin.gov

Tour **Wade House**, a stagecoach inn in the 1800s, and **Wesley J. Jung Carriage Museum**, a collection of almost one hundred horse-drawn vehicles. Also on the state historic site's Greenbush grounds are a blacksmith shop, sawmill, and farm animals. wadehouse.wisconsinhistory.org, (920) 526-3271

Get an introduction to Native American history and artifacts at **Henschel's Indian Museum and Trout Farm**, open Memorial Day to Labor Day. The setting is the Henschel family's rural homestead since 1849. henschelsindianmuseumandtroutfarm.com, (920) 876-3193

Climb the state's tallest wooden observation tower, 80 feet above ground at **Sheboygan Marsh Wildlife Area**, popular for camping, hunting, fishing, canoeing, and foot/disc golf. Add flame-kissed burgers from Three Guys and a Grill at the park's Marsh Lodge. threeguysandagrill.com, (920) 876-2535

See the inside of pretty and rural **All Saints Chapel**, made with fieldstones and plaster in 1951. Episcopal services in the forty-eight-seat church are conducted on summer Sundays, through Labor Day weekend. gracesheboygan.com, (920) 452-9659

"One of the dynamic things is that the big track has stayed the same," says George Bruggenthies, Road America's president until 2019. "That says a lot about the foresight and design of the track. It remains one of the drivers' favorites."

The toughest turn? That might be Canada Corner, where drivers take a hard right after a fast straightaway. Or Corner 5, a 90-degree left-hand turn that also comes off a long straightaway.

Thoughts of Corner 5 refresh another memory: heat of sun, smell of grilled brats, flow of cold beer, squeals from car tires and the crowd. None of that has changed. The setting, for fans, is parklike—open seating on grass and under shade of trees.

Track layout is the same, but crowd access has improved because of the addition of bridges and viewing areas. "It's more like a park than anything," Bruggenthies says. "It's not a dusty oval."

Legendary racers Mario Andretti, Parnelli Jones, David Hobbs, Al Unser, Phil Hill, and Carol Shelby are among those who have competed at Road America. A. J. Foyt crashed there in 1990.

The original track is used about one-half of the year. Newer and smaller tracks (a motorplex, especially for racing karts and hybrid motorcycles, and adventure tracks for ATVs) make it possible for Road America to operate in all seasons.

These are sites for corporate escapes and team-building outings, as well as training grounds for would-be professional racers. Families sled on Road America hills in winter and raise money to fight cancer by running or walking the original track in autumn.

The Karting Experience, for groups of at least six, covers one-half day of training and racing at the motorplex.

Seven adventure trails traverse rock walls and ground holes in Road America's wooded areas. The low-speed adventure requires discipline, balance, and patience as drivers proceed almost at a crawl during some segments.

All the modern options for thrill seekers add to the long-standing reputation of the area, which became a haven for Chicago vacationers—including gamblers and gangsters—in the late 1800s.

Everett Nametz, in Road America's first official program, wrote that the final track design embodied "practically all the normal driving hazards that one might encounter in any section of the country."

Elevation changes several hundred feet from one part of the course to another. The intent, Nametz noted, was to establish a racetrack "with terrain so different from all other racing circuits that after the course was built it would continue to hold the esteem of racing fans and respect of competition drivers down through the years."

Genesee Depot

Population not tracked

Ten Chimneys

tenchimneys.org
(262) 968-4110

What has brought Joel Grey, Phylicia Rashad, Lynn Redgrave, Jason Alexander, and other well-known actors to rural Wisconsin for a part of summer?

Each was a master teacher at Ten Chimneys, a 60-acre estate for artful living and theatrical expression. The National Historic Landmark was a longtime refuge (1920s to 1970s) for Broadway stars Alfred Lunt and Lynn Fontanne, and a destination of inspiration for colleagues.

"Many actors considered Ten Chimneys 'ground zero' for American theater—the place of artistic expression," explains Randy Bryant, Ten Chimneys Foundation president/CEO. That's both then and now.

Charlie Chaplin, George Burns, Helen Hayes, Joan Crawford, Hal Holbrook, and dozens of other stars stayed at Ten Chimneys as the Lunts' guests. "Everybody knew what they stood for," Randy emphasizes: the hosts "perfected acting as we know it today."

FAST FACTS

Alfred Lunt was a Le Cordon Bleu grad-uate, and the actor-chef's recipe was an inspiration for Ten Chimneys Bundt Cake at **Sally's Sweet Shoppe**. The baker makes the cake as a signature dessert for **Cornerstone Café**. The businesses are across the street from each other in Genesee Depot, and the chocolate cake has a ganache center, fudge frosting, white chocolate shavings. sallyssweet shoppe.com, cornerstonegeneseedepot .com, (262) 968-1803, (262) 968-3093

For sale at the Ten Chimneys gift shop is a cookbook of 192 Lunt recipes, illustrated with estate and other pho-tos. Recipes tend to be uncomplicated, and sometimes a mystery ingredient—removed before serving—kept guests guessing.

He added dill pickle slices to canned tomato soup, for example, and whole allspice to simmering clam chowder.

Method acting—when acting doesn't look like acting—was a new concept in the 1920s, when stage shows on Broadway had a season, and TV/film productions were in infancy as entertainment. Instead of talking over each other, actors turned more natural, realistic, conversa-tional, and emotional.

The Lunts' work, on stage and away, earned them a Presidential Medal of Freedom in 1964 and lifetime achievement Tony Award in 1970.

"Plays were written, reworked and honed on the estate during the summer months, before the couple returned" to perform in New York, the National Parks Service states, referring to the Lunts as the "first family" of American theater.

The couple invested in new plays, such as the now-classic *Okla-homa*, and pushed for those they preferred in leading roles, such as Carol Channing in *Hello, Dolly!* Since 2009, up to ten regional-theater actors (each a professional at least 20 years) are chosen for the fel-lowship program, an 8-day immersion led by a master teacher at Ten Chimneys.

EASY DETOUR

Twenty miles north is **Holy Hill Basilica and National Shrine of Mary**, which looms on a hilltop in the **Kettle Moraine State Forest Southern Unit**. For the finest panoramic views, climb 178-step Scenic Tower; open May through October.

Mass (at least one service daily), chapels, and grounds are accessible all year. Carmelite friars care for the 1926 neo-Romanesque basilica, which has stained-glass windows from Munich, hand-carved oak pews, and terrazzo floors. holyhill.com, (262) 628-1838

Art and farm markets, square dances, music tributes, and group dinners liven **Holy Hill Art Farm**, 80 acres and around since the 1860s. A sixth generation of the Loosen family arranges the calendar. Three miles from the basilica. holyhillartfarm.com, (262) 224-6153

Open since 1933 is **Fox and Hounds**, a mostly dinner restaurant that began with a restored, one-room cabin and grew from there. Doesn't matter if you're seated in the Hunt, Oak, Garden, Music, or other room: décor is Old World and inviting. Meals are hearty, and portions generous. Two miles from the basilica. foxandhoundsrestaurant.com, (262) 628-1111

Each master teacher brings a specialty. Spontaneity was Alan Alda's emphasis, and Olympia Dukakis concentrated on Chekov. Open to the public is a week's end, behind-the-scenes look at work done with actors and an interview with the master teacher.

It's all one big reason why Ten Chimneys stays relevant. The destination is not a one-dimensional historic site, and estate tours (offered May to December) go beyond architecture and theater.

"Ten Chimneys is about escapism to a world of gentility," Randy believes. The Lunts "knew the art of living—how to enjoy life instead of just existing."

Original furnishings come from around the world: Delft china, Staffordshire figures, Spanish statues. Possessions turn into artifacts: photos with celebrities long gone, books inscribed by authors from another century.

As newlyweds, the couple lived in a converted chicken coop at the property; his mother and sisters lived in the main house. In 2013, a flock of eighteen White Rock chickens were introduced to the property and gained quite a following. Fans donated more than $68,000 for their well-being, so their coop is more like a house, complete with chandeliers.

At Ten Chimneys is the main house, a cottage, studio, swimming pool, bathhouse, and other ancillary buildings. A program center, open since 2003, makes play readings and history exhibits possible.

Why here? Alfred Lunt was raised in Milwaukee; his family would picnic among these walnut groves and oak savannahs. A truly rural area during his boyhood.

Green Lake

Population 1,001

Greenway House

greenwayhousebandb.com
(920) 379-0033

The Winnebago tribe knew of the lake as Daycholah, a beautiful, mysterious, and magical body of water that seemed to have no bottom. It was a place of spiritual pilgrimage centuries ago, and Native American burial mounds dot the lakeshore.

Green Lake, at 236 feet, is widely touted as the deepest natural inland lake in Wisconsin (Lake Wazee in Jackson County is comparable). On the northern shore is Green Lake, the community, and it is not an average resort town. Greenway House, a bed-and-breakfast inn, is within view of the lake and named after the man who put the town on the map as a vacation destination.

When entrepreneur David Greenway opened Oakwood Hotel in 1867, it was described as the first resort west of Niagara Falls. Four years later, railroad tracks were routed to Green Lake, and that brought travelers from as far away as the East Coast.

FAST FIVE

The 115-guest-room **Heidel House**, an 18-acre lakefront resort that began as a private residence, switched to public lodging in 1945. It is the only public resort that remains in Green Lake. New owners took over in 2019 and spent $11 million to upgrade the property. heidelhouse.com, (920) 807-0300

Oldest golf course in Wisconsin is **Tuscumbia**, around since 1896. The eighteen holes are in a parklike, wooded setting that is next to Heidel House. **Lawsonia**, which opened in 1930, ranks among the nation's top one hundred public courses. The Links and Woodland courses are on the outskirts of Green Lake. tuscumbia.net, (920) 294-3381; lawsonia.com, (920) 294-3320

The lakeside setting of **Norton's** has attracted boaters and supper club fans since 1947. Begin with steamed mussels. End with *schaum* torte. Take comfort near the dining room fireplace or nurse a cocktail on the patio during summer. nortonsgreenlake.com, (920) 294-6577

Four miles west of downtown Green Lake is 900-acre **Green Lake Conference Center**, which organizes Christian-based retreats and accommodates groups up to 1,000. Nonchurch groups are welcome. Look for prayer towers and a restored railroad chapel car on the grounds. Alcohol is not allowed. Hotel suites to dorm-like housing, 220 rooms total. glcc.org, (920) 294-3323

For more about the area: visitgreenlake.com, (920) 294-3231.

The Oakwood sat on 35 acres with at least 1 mile of lakefront and grew from there. During its prime, the resort accommodated 300 people per night, four times its initial capacity.

"It even had its own vineyard and telegraph system," states Oshkosh Public Museum archives. "People were called to dinner with a large Chinese gong" and paid $7 per day for lodging.

Vacationers typically stayed three weeks or longer because it was an ordeal to reach the area, and by 1900 Green Lake was home to five large resort hotels. The resorts pretty much employed the whole town, but they all were made of wood, and some succumbed to fire.

Much vanished by the 1950s as autos nudged out rail travel in popularity. Part of the Oakwood complex was an exception, but it eventually fell into disrepair and by 2012 was demolished.

The same almost happened to Greenway House, an 1880 mansion next to the Oakwood where David Greenway lived with his family until his death in 1905. Then the house sat vacant.

The lack of attention gnawed at Wayne Chaney, a retired attorney and property developer. "Somebody's got to save it," he thought, but almost 10 years passed, and nobody did. So, he and architect Brian Fisher took on the project, investing $500,000 to rehab it.

"We didn't intend to operate a B&B," Wayne says, but "it didn't make sense to renovate the building as a residence because it was too big and needed too much work."

Retained and buffed were original maple floors, fireplaces, stained glass, leaded windows. Added were flowering pear trees on the grounds and private bathrooms with spa tubs in the seven guest accommodations.

QUICK DETOUR

Ten miles north of Green Lake is **Russell Moccasin Company**, Berlin, population 5,571. The family business since 1898 has made handsome, customized footwear one pair at a time. Customers choose from more than one hundred types of leather, some from exotic animals. Boots for the outdoors buff—hunter to hiker— are a specialty. Many styles, for men and women, available. russellmoccasin.com, (920) 361-2252

Guest bedrooms are named after Green Lake's big resorts of the 1880s, contain nostalgic photos from the era, and are within a glance of the lake that still lures travelers today. Instead of an eyesore, Greenway House is a tribute to the past and beacon of hope for the future.

Johnsonville

Population not tracked

Johnsonville Marketplace

**johnsonvillemarketplace.com
(920) 453-5678**

Throughout Sheboygan County is a long and passionate love for bratwurst. We grill the links for summer picnics and subzero football tailgating. We debate how to best prepare the traditional pork sausage and consider it proof of German heritage.

Some butcher shops fill sausage casings with other ingredients—chicken, meat blends, jalapeños, apricots, sauerkraut, cheese, pineapple, horseradish—and still call 'em brats. When is a brat not a brat? That's a discussion for another time.

The brat fry—outdoor grilling and maybe a little shack for ordering—is a popular fund-raiser for churches, schools, 4-H clubs, and nonprofit causes. Perhaps as common as bake sales in this part of rural Wisconsin.

Johnsonville Sausage, the nation's largest producer of bratwurst, provides the exclamation point for all this pride and identity. The fourth-generation enterprise sells meat products in at least forty-five countries and all fifty states. It is one of the food industry's top companies that remains family owned.

Headquarters for production is less than 1 mile from a one-road community where the business began. It's a town so small that all might easily fit into the corporate

FAST FACT

Across from the original Johnsonville Meats (replaced by a smoked meats facility) is century-old **Laack's Tavern and Ballroom**, whose basement with hardwood floor was on the long-ago playing circuit for Dick Jurgens, Guy Lombardo, and other nationally known orchestras.

Although public dances with polkas and waltzes have dwindled, Laack's retains a solid fan base and over decades built a reputation as a popular community meeting space and wedding reception site.

The building was sold in 2022, after four generations of Laack family ownership, but new co-owner Susan Radke intends to uphold traditions. Her **HUB Studio Café** (coffeehouse, cafe, and art boutique) also has been moved into the structure, which has an attached and long-shuttered shopfront. thehubcoffee.com, (920) 893-9000

campus. To coincide with the sausage maker's seventy-fifth year, Johnsonville Marketplace opened in 2020 to give brat fans a reason to sniff out the company's birthplace.

In 1945, Johnsonville Meats was a mom-and-pop butcher shop that two hardworking and frugal couples—Ralph and Alice Stayer, Carl and Anna Hirsch—bought for $11,500 in a village of German descent, along the Sheboygan River. The men learned the trade of meat processing while working in Milwaukee but dreamed of doing business their way, on their own.

Sheboygan County had lots of butchers who made sausage back then. The site of Johnsonville Meats was already in business 50 years when ownership changed, but this no longer would be business as usual. Instead of using meat scraps in sausage, the new owners' Old World family recipe relied on better-quality pork and spices.

By the 1970s, "Big Taste from a Small Town" was a Johnsonville Sausage slogan, and company size mushroomed. Community size didn't: Johnsonville is big enough for a volunteer fire department and 4-H club

(Johnsonville Hustlers) but not a post office or gas station. It has no stop signs or sidewalks.

The German settlement was known as Schnappsville (it had at least three saloons) until renamed in the 1860s, after President Andrew Johnson. A riverside "Schnappsville Park" sign acknowledges that piece of the past.

Johnsonville—the community—is surrounded by farmland and quiet, with notable exceptions. Polka dancing begins at noon at the annual Sausage Fest, on the Sunday after July Fourth. Highlight of the annual Pretzel Bender is a short but lively midnight parade through town. Busloads come for Fasching Feast, before Lenten season begins.

Tours of Johnsonville—the sausage company—aren't possible, but Johnsonville Marketplace is a place to buy about anything the brand represents. Dozens of meat products—including new items and others not found in grocery stores—are one line of inventory.

Made just for this business is Grumpy Grandpa beer, a Potosi Brewing Company product that is a loving tribute to Johnsonville Sausage founder Ralph Stayer.

Anything eaten or used to produce a brat fry—condiments to barbecue grills—is sold. So are other Wisconsin-made foods and beverages. On apparel are sometimes-sassy messages, such as "You're the Wurst" and "Don't Call Me a Weenie."

Delayed by the pandemic was the opening of a paved patio, complete with grills, for local charities to conduct brat fry fund-raisers.

Kohler

Population 2,195

The American Club Resort Hotel

theamericanclub.com
(800) 344-2838

A better life: That is what immigrants sought when leaving European homelands and taking treacherous ocean voyages more than one century ago. They arrived in America with big dreams but certainly no guarantees.

In Kohler is a rags-to-riches, real-time illustration of the best of what was possible.

The American Club in Kohler opened in 1918 as dormitory housing for nearly 150 immigrant factory workers, right across from Kohler Company, the plumbing manufacturer that sold hog scalders/water troughs as bathtubs in 1883.

Today the dormitory is a historic hotel that has earned a five-diamond rating every year since 1985. **Kohler Waters Spa** ranks among the best in the world; many therapeutic services involve water that flows through contemporary Kohler-made fixtures.

Kohler golf courses—designed by Pete Dye—are among the finest, too. **Whistling Straits**, 10 miles north of Kohler and along Lake Michigan,

hosted the 2020 Ryder Cup, team play for the best golfers in the United States and Europe. These two courses and Kohler's two **Black Wolf Run** courses also have hosted PGA championships and U.S. Women's Opens.

The area's reputation for golf excellence is long standing. *Golf Digest* in the late 1990s declared Sheboygan County one of the best places to play golf in the world.

Such praise made my eyes widen back then because the part of Sheboygan County where I grew up was all about frugal and hard-working farmers. They didn't golf because they were planting, haying, combining, picking corn, and milking cows. Our idea of splurging was a double brat on a hardroll during a summer Firemen's Picnic, not a multicourse dinner at The American Club.

A big reason why Kohler quality—in plumbing products and hospitality—stays steady is because of the work ethic and dedication that Sheboygan County's salt-of-the-earth workers pass on to younger generations.

I doubt that many people, before the turn of this century, pictured Kohler with an international reputation for golf. But this wasn't the first time the Kohler family proved naysayers wrong.

When Austrian immigrant John Michael Kohler decided long ago to build a plumbing fixture factory on 21 acres of farmland, 4 miles from the nearest city, the local newspaper called it "Kohler's Folly." That's where the family's New World dream persisted, despite challenges.

The factory was rebuilt before it opened, having burned during construction. The founder and two sons died around then, too, leaving a third son—Walter Kohler—to persevere.

What he chose to provide to workers from Germany and beyond was a place to live as well as work and a way of life that would lead to U.S. citizenship. Both the brick factory and Tudor-style American Club were part of a 50-year plan for a tidy company town, designed by the Olmstead Brothers (also responsible for Central Park in New York City) to prevent haphazard community growth.

ARTS/INDUSTRY

Outdoors at The American Club, to commemorate the structure's centennial, is a sculpture of a boy with an American flag. The cast-iron work is called *The Immigrant* and was created by Stephen Paul Day of New Orleans, one of the hundreds of artists-in-residence at Kohler Company since an arts/industry program began in 1974.

Artists arrive from around the world, using industrial materials and equipment to create items that would not be possible in their own studios. They typically leave behind one piece of artwork; some are large-scale, outdoor sculptures in Kohler.

Artists interact with foundry and/or pottery factory employees to create the art; the setting fosters an appreciation for each other's work. A three-month residency includes housing, a stipend, materials, technical assistance, and 24-hour access to factory studio space. jmkac.org/arts-industry

About 200 men worked at the Kohler foundry and enameling factory, making bathtubs to faucets, when The American Club opened. Workers paid $27.50 per month for room and board: Their dormitory-style lodging was simple but clean with in-house access to a cafeteria, bowling alley, tap room, and barbershop.

"The Club was never intended to earn a profit," explained a 1920 booklet about Kohler. "It was intended to furnish the men with a place where they can be comfortable, healthy and happy. No man can do his work well if he has not a good place to live, good food to eat, clean surroundings and a chance to enjoy life."

Trees and gardens were plentiful then and now. Retail, industrial, and residential areas still look like they belong together architecturally.

As automobiles became more common, the 4-mile work commute to Kohler no longer seemed cumbersome. Single men married and started families in homes of their own.

Worker housing no longer was needed, so Herbert Kohler Jr.—grandson of the factory founder—decided in 1978 to turn The American Club into luxury lodging. Eyes widened again.

Each of 241 guest accommodations at the hotel is devoted to a famous person, so no two are identical in decor. What stays the same? The setting, looks, and attitude.

Framed photos from simpler times grace hotel walls, especially near The Horse and Plow, a classy-casual pub with microbrews, creative burgers, fireplace, and big-screen TVs. Most formal is the Immigrant

ART PRESERVE

Open since 2021 and just east of Kohler is the $40 million **Art Preserve**, the world's first museum devoted to artist-built environments. Most works were created by people with little or no art training. For example:

Loy Bowlin, a poor man in Mississippi, called himself "The Original Rhinestone Cowboy" and immersed his home in glitz and bling. Emery Blagdon filled a large shed in rural Nebraska with his vivid paintings and shiny mobiles, referring to it as a "healing machine."

About 20,000 objects are rotated in and out of Art Preserve dark storage, and items come from as far away as India. Admission is free to the 38-acre site, a satellite campus for **John Michael Kohler Arts Center** in downtown Sheboygan. jmkac.org/art-preserve, (920) 453-0346

Kohler Foundation is a global leader in identifying, preserving, and securing long-term stewards for neglected art environments. Several sites are in Wisconsin, including **James Tellen Woodland Sculpture Garden**, 8 miles southeast of Kohler; thirty-some concrete statues were made by a furniture factory worker. wanderingwisconsin.org

Restaurant, where jackets are required for men and each of six dining rooms pays tribute to a segment of ethnic heritage.

A second 50-year plan for Kohler (by the Frank Lloyd Wright Foundation) stays true to what was proposed a century ago. Yet growth is allowed in new ways, especially as it pertains to wellness options (golf simulators and private lessons, many classes of yoga weekly) and expanded water treatments at the spa.

Also in the Destination Kohler brand are casual to fine-dining restaurants; the Carriage House, lodging above the spa; Inn on Woodlake, with suites as large as four bedrooms; and five secluded, finely appointed cabins.

Available at The American Club are self-guided and guided hotel history and garden tours. Kohler Company began offering factory tours in the 1920s; retired factory workers lead free, two-hour, weekday tours. Reservations are required. destinationkohler.com, (920) 457-8000

IN THE NEIGHBORHOOD

In the lower level of **Kohler Design Center** (marketplace for stylish Kohler products, where toilets and bathtubs are arranged like fine art), is a free museum devoted to all things Kohler. Think cast-iron plows and old-time bathtubs to foundry-made art and explanatory videos about hospitality development. kohler.com, (920) 457-3699

For sale in the hotel gift shop and nearby **Shops at Woodlake**: Kohler Original Recipe Chocolates, boxed chocolates that look like little jewels and small-batch candy bars. The line began with Terrapins, a refined version of the better-known pecan-caramel-chocolate turtle candy. Herb Kohler's love of fine chocolate seeped into liquor, too, through dark chocolate and chocolate mint brandies. kohlerchocolates.com

Open daily for guided tours is **Waelderhaus**, an architectural tribute to the Alpine area of Austria that is the homeland of Kohler family ances-tors. The name means "house in the woods," and the building is a mix of stained glass, wrought iron, carved wood, and imported tapestries. kohlerfoundation.org/waelderhaus, (920) 453-2851

Three miles east of Kohler is **Bookworm Gardens**, where whimsical artwork pays homage to beloved children's books in each of seventy-plus gardens. Exam-ple: near a small bridge with railings of woven ropes are statues of waddling waterfowl, a nod to the book *Make Way for Ducklings*. Admission is free, most paths are wheelchair accessible, and an expansion means that the 7.5-acre site will triple in size. Open May through October. bookwormgardens.org

Two miles north of Kohler is **The Blind Horse**, a restaurant and winery on 7 acres of a former farm whose workhorse, Birdy, was blind. Musi-cians perform seasonally on the roomy outdoor patio, making it a pop-ular gathering spot. Dinner is served in an 1880s farmhouse. theblindhorse.com, (920) 467-8599

Closest state park: **Kohler-Andrae**, where windswept sand dunes and beach follow Lake Michigan shoreline. Black River Marsh Boardwalk is wheelchair accessible. More challenging: the two-mile Dunes Cordwalk. dnr.wisconsin.gov, (920) 451-4080

Mount Calvary

Population 548

Wisconsin's Holyland

With the arrival of spring comes the promise of renewal, revival, and—especially for Christians—resurrection and rebirth as Easter approaches.

It was that way for German farm immigrants in the mid-1800s, too, and hundreds brought to the Midwest their prospects for prosperity and the faith to be at peace with whatever was out of their hands.

You'll find much evidence of those high yet humble hopes in **Wisconsin's Holyland**, where ten Catholic churches in or near mostly unincorporated towns—such as Jericho, St. Peter, Johnsburg, St. Joe—have long dotted the quiet, agricultural landscape within northern Fond du Lac and southern Calumet counties.

"Many times the church was built first, and the community developed around it," notes *Breaking Bread in the Holyland*, a booklet about the area's history. "Although some churches have been remodeled, and the use of some converted from places of worship, the spiritual impact of the entire Holyland remains strong."

FAST FACT

The Holyland and White Lightnin', a doctoral dissertation by John W. Jenkins (a native of Pipe, population not tracked), described the area as "a key producer of illicit liquor" during Prohibition.

"The agricultural depression of the 1920s" and subsequent Great Depression "opened the ears and barns of local dairy farmers, mink farmers and cheese factory owners to the lucrative brewing, distilling and selling of illegal booze," he wrote, "to provide support for their families" and find a use for grain surpluses.

At the heart of the Holyland is Mount Calvary and its 170-student St. Lawrence Seminary High School, which opened in 1860 as Convent Latin School. Teen boys from around the world attend the boarding school, but not all are studying to become a priest.

Saint Isidore the Farmer Parish is among the Holyland churches that are served by Capuchin Franciscan friars. Shuttered since 2012 is Our Lady of Mount Carmel convent, established in Mount Calvary in 1852. Within town are Notre Dame, Maria, St. Anthony, and Church Streets.

In unincorporated St. Joe, a sturdy Catholic school sits vacant. Five rural parish schools were consolidated into one by 1985 and today are known as Holyland Catholic School.

It is not unusual for Holyland churches to share the services of a priest and not unprecedented for that priest to be of an advanced age. Masses occur in rotation.

TWO ANIMAL HAVENS

At the outskirts of Mount Calvary is **Cristo Rey Ranch**, a 300-animal menagerie of peacocks to potbellied pigs, horses to cats, alpacas to emus. These creatures share 120 acres with a Catholic convent, **Villa Loretto** nursing home and **Villa Rosa**, assisted-living apartments.

Pet therapy is a part of programming for elders. Ranch staff work with at-risk youth, too, and arrange farm tours for groups. For sale at the gift shop are handicrafts, some made with wool from the farm's animals. cristoreyranch.org, (920) 753-1053

Four miles south is **Holyland Donkey Haven**, a nonprofit refuge with rehab for donkeys rescued from abuse, neglect, or abandonment. Sponsors help pay for the care of those that can't be adopted. holylanddonkeyhaveninc.com, (920) 915-2873

IN THE NEIGHBORHOOD

The Holyland is east of Lake Winnebago, the largest inland lake in Wisconsin at 220 square miles. No body of water in the world has a higher recreational harvest of sturgeon, and the annual winter spearing season for this ancient species is possible because of smart and ongoing fish management.

Winnebago's east side is big on agriculture, and a few farms welcome visitors.

Three generations have planted sixteen types of apple trees at **Heritage Orchard**, overlooking the lake and north of Brothertown, population 201. Pluck pumpkin patches, too, and buy apple-centric merchandise in autumn. heritageorchardwi.com, (920) 849-2158

LaClare Family Creamery, near Malone, population not tracked, produces award-winning cheeses with milk from farm goats: Evalon, a gouda-style cheese, was first in 2011 World Championship Cheese competition. Brunch, lunch, or take a class at the farmstead café. Shop for soaps, lotions, and caramels—all contain goat milk. Tour on your own or with a guide. laclarefamilycreamery.com, (920) 670-0051

The Little Farmer, west of Johnsburg, population not tracked, has animals to feed and pet, a playground and autumn corn maze, apple house with pecks and pies, coffeehouse and gift shop (in a converted farmhouse). mytlf.com, (920) 921-4784

A few miles south of the Holyland are two more notable farm stops. **Ledgerock Distillery** uses limestone-filtered water and the farm's corn; sip and notice the nearby wind turbine farm. **Kelley Country Creamery** wins international awards for its ice creams, made within view of the family's 1861 farm. ledgerockdistillery.com, (920) 238-9588; kelleycountrycreamery.com, (920) 923-1715

Closest state park: **High Cliff**, near Sherwood. Scoot up the Niagara Escarpment's limestone cliffs for hiking, beautiful Lake Winnebago views, and to find limekiln ruins, Native American effigy mounds. dnr.wisconsin.gov, (920) 989-1106

Listen and look for sweet little surprises, such as the unexpected chiming of church bells or finding weathered but still glorious statuettes on tombstones and pillars. It is not difficult to sense great congregational pride while driving this area's tidy hills, walking its well-kept church cemeteries, or having the good luck to see the inside of a gorgeous little sanctuary.

For me, the latter happened because of good timing and goodwill. While leaving the hilltop grounds of **St. Mary's** in—take a guess—Marytown (population not tracked), a church member was arriving.

He rolled down his window to inquire, "Want to see the inside? I have to check the furnace."

While expressing my delight at the immaculate and ornate nave, he suggested looking from the choir loft. "You should see it decorated at Christmastime," he added. "Just beautiful."

He was a church member and rightfully proud of that fact.

The first St. Mary's—also known as Blessed Virgin Mary Catholic Church—was made of logs in 1849 and burned in 1880. Fire destroyed the second parish, too, so the third was built with stone.

Mass is held at least once a day in the rural Holyland. Check ourladyoftheholyland.org for times and locations.

Breaking Bread in the Holyland also introduces the area's supper clubs, "the ideal place to break bread." Why link the two? It historically was not uncommon to find one near the other.

"After Sunday Mass many adults would flock to the supper clubs for brunch, drinks and a challenging game of cards," the booklet observes. "In later years, going to Mass on a Saturday night and then to the supper club was the norm for hard-working" rural couples.

Download the booklet at travelcalumet.com. Visit **Malone Area Heritage Museum**, Malone, for oral histories and artifacts from the era. facebook.com/malonearea, (920) 579-2738

Count long-standing **Schwarz Supper Club** in St. Anna—known for steak-seafood combos, generous portions, and leisurely dining—among the state's most popular. Start with onion rings, hand cut and hand breaded. What began as a one-room tavern now can serve more than 700 per night. schwarzsupperclub.com, (920) 894-3598

Pardeeville

Population 2,074

Pardeeville Watermelon Festival

pardeevillewatermelonfestival.com

My guy argues that all small-town Wisconsin festivals are pretty much the same: bands, beer tent, burgers, and brats. Maybe a parade, car show, arts/crafts fair, and carnival games/rides, too.

That's not the case in Pardeeville, where the first Saturday after Labor Day is devoted to watermelon. Everybody eats as much as they want, for free. Kids play endearing, watermelon-themed games that are homemade. Carvers in two hours turn whole melons into whimsical art. Gardeners haul in abnormally large melons for gawking.

Perhaps most significant are the U.S. Watermelon Speed-Eating and Seed-Spitting Championships. Records in fifteen categories are destined to be broken. Winners get bragging rights but little else.

Native son Clark Hodgson in 1988 set the men's open record for spitting a seed 61 feet, 3 inches. Guy Berst of Portage in 1985 ate a wedge of melon in 4 seconds to set the record for speed eaters who are ages 12 to 16. Other records were upended much more recently.

Speed eating and seed spitting were the foundation of the festival since its beginning in 1968, the result of brainstorming about how to

QUICK TAKES

Two other examples of towns that don't involve alcohol in major annual events:

Alto 4-H and Farm Bureau Fair lasts only two days and happens during mid-week in August, making it the shortest and smallest annual summertime fair in Wisconsin. A beloved tradition since the 1950s in Alto (population 166), Fond du Lac County, and hundreds of volunteers make it happen. The fair's chili and sloppy joe recipes haven't changed since the beginning. Grilled cheddar sandwiches use Saputo Cheese, the area's biggest employer. The top pie maker gets $100. Judges are generous with blue-ribbon awards. Free admission. It's like a big family reunion. altofair.com, (920) 948-9307

Nobody argues when St. Peter's Evangelical Lutheran Church, Lebanon (population 1,587), says its annual **Christmas cookie sale** is largest in Wisconsin. Children, senior citizens, church members, and nonmembers work together to make and bake 150 kinds of cookies, all carefully decorated, weighing in at 3,000 pounds total. Ingredients arrive by semi tractor-trailer. From-scratch soups and *Kranzkuchen* (a wreath-shaped coffee cake) also sold by the Dodge County congregation with German roots. Admission is by entry number on the first Saturday of December. Shut-ins get leftovers. stpetersoflebanonwi.org, (920) 925-3547

make Pardeeville better known and distinguish it from other lovely little waterfront burgs. Chandler Park, which juts into Park Lake near downtown, remains the perfect backdrop.

Most every community, large and small, comes up with a way and reason to gather. The most diligent elevate a symbol of local identity simultaneously. Pardeeville efforts began as watermelons grew in abundance.

"We'd contract with local farmers to grow an acre (of melons) for us," recalls Todd Hepler, a festival organizer, circuit court judge, and native of the area. Worries escalated if weather challenged the growing season: Would melons ripen in time? Would there be enough? Would they taste good?

Locale remains agricultural, but now organizers simply accept a donation of 150 watermelons per year. For a while, the festival lasted more than one day, complete with bands, water-ski shows, boat races, and water battles between firefighters.

The event is unusual—for Wisconsin, at least—because no beer is sold. Early on, the decision was made to be alcohol free and family friendly. It's not about making more money by changing the day's personality.

"The festival was born in the same year I was," Todd says. "I wanted that legacy for my daughters," now teenagers. When the gathering almost faded away a few years ago, a new group of volunteers stepped forward—including him—to rejuvenate it.

"Keeping volunteers involved is a challenge for all small towns," and this one has a strong but small core. Todd saw activities for children as key to the festival's future, so he began building games with a water-melon theme.

Games had dwindled to four or five choices, "nothing you couldn't see in your own home." That expanded to around two dozen cheery tests of luck or skill, a Watermelon Midway where kids spin a six-foot-tall melon wheel, plop disks into an oversized Plinko-like board, and toss hoops onto the top of wooden melon slices.

High school groups operate the games and split profits with the festival, getting $800 in 2021. "We don't put out all (games available) because we need volunteers to run them," Todd says.

It's all in good fun, as long as you abide by the rules for those pre-mier melon contests. For example:

"Official seeds will be provided. No one will be permitted to use their own seed."

"Contestants who accidentally swallow seeds while sucking in air prior to seed launch will be given one extra seed."

And, for denture wearers: "Distance seed travels is the only thing that counts. Poly-grip available on request."

When speed eating, quickness matters but "certain emphasis will also be placed on neatness, lack of burping and certain other competi-tive courtesies."

"Height, weight or size of mouth shall not prevent any individual from competing," but professional tobacco spitters should stay away.

Regardless of category, sponsors are not held responsible "for the after-effects of seeds swallowed by any contestant."

Princeton

Population 1,267

Princeton Flea Market

princetonwi.com
(920) 295-3877

When Mike Jacobi took over flea market management in 1982, there was clean-up work to be done. Some vendors were arriving too early for the weekly, outdoor sale on Saturdays. They'd camp out on Friday night, to stake out a space.

It wasn't necessarily a peaceful bunch: some drank too much and fought with other vendors who grew to feel entitled about where to set up shop. Mike decided to not let anybody into Princeton City Park until 6 a.m., when vendors' vehicles were admitted in the order they arrived and lined up.

"After a month, things settled down," he says, and it probably helped that each got a ticket for a free doughnut and coffee. Free coffee continues as a vendor perk. Crowds disperse at 1 p.m.

In the park is room for 172 vendors. Up to 150 will pay to reserve a space for the entire season ($500 for twenty-six weeks in 2021). Others get in on a daily rate ($35 in 2021). What each sells is a hodgepodge but

a lot different than 1975, when a handful of folks converged on a little street downtown to sell antiques, tools, and "rummage stuff."

Mike says details weren't memorable enough to document, but the market grew steadily from there to become one of the state's longest running and best known, especially for a community this size. At its peak, in the 1990s, he had up to fifty vendors on a waiting list for seasonal space and an annual turnover of maybe ten vendors.

We chat on a drizzly morning in summer, which cuts the sales force to about fifty dealers. How much does rain affect turnout? Mike shrugs: if you sell books, you might stay away. If you sell plants, you don't care as much.

He points out a husband and wife who are Amish and sell bakery. Nods at another who is a longtime grower of plants, especially mums on this day. A Hmong family has driven 100 miles to sell veggies. A woman

THE PORTER FACTOR

Tracy Porter, from the area, developed a line of artsy-chic home furnishings—Stonehouse Farm Goods—that helped establish Princeton as a small town that's big on boutiques and style. Her clientele included Neiman Marcus and Nordstrom in the 1990s.

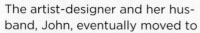

The artist-designer and her husband, John, eventually moved to California, but a subtle impact remains. Gone is Tracy Porter, the shop, in downtown Princeton—but the space is under development as **Parlor**, a boutique hotel. parlorhotel.com

Also within two blocks of Water Street: **Daiseye**, handcrafted décor with repurposed materials; **Green 3**, apparel and furnishings made with sustainable fibers; **Twister**, espresso café with gifts; and art galleries.

Horseradish Kitchen + Market serves unconventional snacks and lunches, such as Korean nachos (with kimchi). **Renard's European Bakeshop** sells fancy pastries and artisan breads. **Knickerbocker Landing** serves craft cocktails in an 1880 stone building with carved oak bar. princetonwi.com, (920) 295-3877

whose farm is nearby has, since the beginning, sold dried flowers and bedding plants; she also sells pumpkins in season.

No one—by market rule—sells animals, guns, fireworks, alcohol, or knock-offs of high-end brands. Political booths are banned, too: "I had a vendor come in a while back with a booth devoted to politics," Mike explains. "He got weird and obnoxious. Had to be removed before the market ended that day."

Local nonprofits take turns operating the food stand and benefiting from sales. A menu of burgers, hot dogs, and brats is typical. Some add baked goods, chili, pulled pork, walking tacos.

"I grew old here," says vendor Cathy Fenner, who sells antiques and perennial plants. She adds a granddaughter's sedum gardens, arranged in little containers.

With her husband, Jerry ("the driver and hauler"), they have sold at the market since it began, rising at 3 a.m. to make the 75-mile drive to Princeton. The couple married six years before those treks started, and on Sundays they head 100 miles to a flea market in a different direction. "It's kept us busy on weekends," Jerry says. An understatement.

The thrill of the hunt, for this vendor and others, goes both ways. You're on the road to find new merchandise as well as sell it. A daughter adds internet marketing. "Good thing," Cathy says. "We don't have a computer."

IN THE NEIGHBORHOOD

At **Mecan River Outfitters**, 3 miles west, are 10 miles of trails for biking and hiking. Pay a trail fee to roam on your own. Rent a canoe or kayak for 2 hours or longer. Book a guided hunt on 500 private acres. No need to leave as the day ends: dine on hearty fare at the lodge and nurse a nightcap in front of the 35-foot-tall fireplace before heading to a rustic cabin or cozy lodge bedroom. mecanriveroutfitters.com, (920) 295-3439

Waterloo

Population 3,492

Trek Bicycle Corp.

trekbikes.com
(920) 478-2191

At the edge of town, close to woods and farm fields, is headquarters for the world's largest maker of bicycles sold by specialty retailers. Free, weekly, 1-hour tours introduce company history, bike design, and bike racing via Trek products.

Trek is the kind of company where employees dress casually, are rewarded for bicycling to work, and have easy access to a well-equipped exercise room. Visitor parking signs reveal a biting sense of humor, as in, "Your car probably wishes it was a bike" and "Visiting? This is your spot. Working? Go somewhere else."

Trek-Segafredo, the company's road racing teams, compete globally. That includes Tour de France, the grueling summer event in twenty-one stages over twenty-three days.

TREK TRAVEL

A subset of Trek Bicycle Corp. designs vacation itineraries—ways to ride around parts of the world on your own or in a small group, at an athletic or leisurely pace. Your choice.

Trek Travel destinations are big on natural beauty, especially throughout Europe and U.S. national parks. Efforts began in 2002 and trips arranged as far away as New Zealand and Japan. Excursions provide an up-close and sometimes luxurious look at another landscape and/or culture. Riding terrain will depend upon the destination chosen. Groups are no larger than sixteen.

Support staff and tour guides are prepared to accommodate couples whose bike-riding skills and interests don't match. One can sweat up a mountain while the other begins shopping or wine tasting after a shorter stint of riding. Tool along on an e-bike or go for a full-gear, day-long workout.

Airfare to the destination is not included, but lodging, most meals—and use of a Trek bike—can be a part of the deal. trektravel.com, (866) 464-8735

LIFE BEFORE TREK

Long before Trek, Waterloo was known for producing sausage and sauerkraut. That is why **Weiner and Kraut Day** remains an end-of-summer tradition that began in 1960. The annual September festival at Firemen's Park began as a nod to two major and local businesses, Van Holten's (whose focus is pickle production today) and Kress Packing Company (no longer in business).

A parade of dachshunds is customary at Weiner and Kraut Day. Other dog breeds are welcome. Add a 5-kilometer run, car show, beer garden, bands, and sports tourneys. Proceeds benefit local charities. waterloowi.us, (920) 478-3025

Most Trek bikes are made in other countries, but the company says every bike used by its international teams is built and inspected in Waterloo. Carbon technology produces ultralight but strong road bike frames that exceed aerospace standards for manufacturing. Trek produces mountain bikes, bikes for kids, and electric bikes.

An atrium collection shows how Trek bike models have changed with time. Tours introduce the on-site bike design studio or other behind-the-scenes work areas. Rugged outdoor trails, secluded from the average person's view, are used for bike testing and occasional events with rigorous challenges.

These trails are ground zero for autumn Trek CX Cup competition, one of nine races in the World Cup Cyclocross series. Most of the others

ANCIENT HISTORY, MYSTERY

Twelve miles southeast is **Aztalan**, remnants of a significant but mysterious Native American settlement for 300 years, until abandoned in the year 1200. Massive religious mounds remain on 172 acres, and a state marker describes the ancient village as "a unique blend of native and exotic cultures."

The Crawfish River site, considered a prehistoric Aztec community, is both a National Historic Landmark and a Wisconsin state park. dnr.wisconsin.gov, (608) 873-9695

On a museum campus in the town of Aztalan (population 1,382), north of the state park, are seven pioneer-era structures that include a Baptist church and one-room schoolhouse. lakemillsaztalanhistory.com, (920) 728-2685

happen in Europe. Although World Cup Waterloo racers are elite athletes, amateurs use the same track to compete in their own gritty races during the weekend.

Trek in October hosts National Interscholastic Cycling Association state championships for high school mountain bikers. The Trek 100, every summer since 1990, through bike riding has raised millions to fight childhood cancer and related blood disorders.

Trek, in South African language, means "long journey," and the company's path began in a barn near Waterloo in 1976. The first road racing model came out in 1982, and Lance Armstrong signed on with Trek in 1997, two years before winning the first of seven Tour de France titles that later were stripped because of a doping investigation.

Williams Bay

Population 2,953

Yerkes Observatory

yerkesobservatory.org

Most people visit Geneva Lake for a vacation, but astronomers know of it as a special place to work and think beyond this galaxy.

Welcome to the birthplace of modern astrophysics and the world's largest telescope until 1908. The 20-ton device with 40-inch-wide lens, dedicated in 1897, remains the world's largest refracting telescope.

Experts describe Yerkes as America's first professional observatory devoted—from its start—to mapping the sky by studying the physical nature of nebulas, stars, planets, and galaxies.

Count Albert Einstein, Carl Sagan, and Nobel Prize winners among those who have found their way to the observatory. Edwin Hubble—for whom the Hubble Space Telescope is named—studied at Yerkes to earn a PhD in 1917. A century later, Yerkes engineers built the HAWC (high-resolution airborne wideband camera) for NASA.

The University of Chicago owned the facility until it was donated to the nonprofit Yerkes Future Foundation. Public tours ended temporarily, until after the pandemic, when they were resumed by reservation.

Why is the observatory here? Williams Bay was close enough to Chicago because of train routes, yet far enough away from industrial pollution that would cloud telescopic observations.

Why didn't others create bigger refracting telescopes? Favored technology changed soon after the huge Yerkes telescope was in place. Astronomers switched to reflecting telescopes that were less expensive to produce.

Yerkes "was intended to be used by a group of top-flight scientists, working more or less independently, to unravel the secrets of the universe we live in—'who we are, where we came from, where we are going'—on the cosmic scale," astronomer Donald Osterbrock wrote in his 1997 book *Yerkes Observatory 1892–1950*.

LAKESHORE PATH

Surrounding Geneva Lake are zillions of dollars in mansions that are occupied only seasonally or occasionally, but anybody can stroll all or a part of the lake's 21-mile perimeter for an inkling of the good life. There is no cost, outside of tired muscles.

The shoreline path, like the architecture it shadows, is far from uniform. Pavement morphs from brick to jagged concrete, recycled rubber, stone mosaics, dirt, and gravel. Stairs and twists lead to ledges, for sale signs, bonfire pits, private beaches, and maybe a lemonade stand.

The path is public, but much of the property is private. What is lacking are clues about who lives here. Rarely are properties identified publicly, but Wrigley, Swift, Sears, Maytag, and other Chicago industrialists figure into lakeshore history. Local businesses sell pocket guides that describe points of interest.

Here are distances and average walk times: Lake Geneva to Williams Bay, 7 miles, 3 hours; Williams Bay to Fontana, 3.5 miles, 1.5 hours; Fontana to Linn Pier, 5.5 miles, 2 hours; Linn Pier to Big Foot State Park, 3.3 miles, 1.2 hours; Big Foot State Park to Lake Geneva, 2.5 miles, 1 hour.

The time it actually takes depends upon weather and stride. Use a restroom before beginning a shoreline walk. The steepest stretches of terrain are between Fontana and Big Foot State Park.

Want advice about how much of your hike remains? Ask a local: they are the ones who don't carry backpacks, water bottles, or cameras.

For more about the area: visitlakegeneva.com, (262) 248-4416.

WATER WAYS

No ground shuttle transports shoreline walkers, so that means walking all around Geneva Lake, backtracking on your path, parking cars at the start and end points of a hike, or arranging a boat ride back to the starting point.

One popular approach: walk from Lake Geneva to Williams Bay, where **Lake Geneva Cruise Line** stops at predetermined times/dates. Years ago, I caught a brunch cruise, complete with tour narration, en route to my starting point. The trick is to arrive at the pickup point on time, so stay on pace.

In the fleet are boats with open and enclosed cabins that seat up to 225.

Most unusual is the cruise company's summer **U.S. Mailboat Tour**: an agile intern repeatedly jumps from the boat as it slows from one dock to another, sprinting to mailboxes on piers, then leaping back onboard. The narrated tours last almost 3 hours and involve up to sixty homes (of the 1,200-some lakeside docks).

Tours of **Black Point Estate**, an 1888 blufftop getaway with thirteen bedrooms, begin with a narrated boat ride. The estate, a state historic site, is unusual because five generations of the same family occupied it before structure and furnishings were donated to the state of Wisconsin.

In December, **Santa Cruise** passengers see animated displays and the holiday lights of shoreline homes from the comfort of a heated and enclosed boat. In warmer weather, cruises with a meal, ice cream, cocktails, music, or straightforward narration are frequent. cruiselakegeneva.com, (262) 248-6206

The site remains a notable destination for those who appreciate space exploration, but the uninitiated historically have been welcome, too. Dennis Kois, executive director at Yerkes, considers the observatory "one of the Midwest's best-kept secrets," one with potential to "build scientific literacy" and the average person's understanding of astronomy.

Much about the 50-acre campus is grand, inside and out. Grounds were designed by landscape architect Frederick Olmsted, responsible for New York City's Central Park and other major urban footprints.

The Beaux Arts observatory, a brown brick building, contains numerous embellishments—cornices, textured columns of terra-cotta—and is big on symmetry. The first floor is raised. Windows are arched. The Great Dome is 90 feet in diameter.

"Nowhere in the world can claim this amount of important astronomy discoveries," Walt Chadick, director of programs, says of Yerkes. "So, we begin with that," but he predicts a future that encompasses interdisciplinary interests.

A goal is to have all three Yerkes telescopes working and available for viewing nights and classes. Additional opportunities to educate and engage will involve the arts, architecture, apiary science, and more.

"This will be much more than a science research facility," Walt says. "We hope to bring sculptors, poets, fiction writers, painters, photographers, performance artists, and creators from diverse fields to work and exhibit on our campus."

An 1896 house on the grounds is being restored as lodging for visiting scientists and artists. Five miles of walking trails will crisscross the grounds and woods.

The campus is named after the guy who paid $400,000 for it: Charles Tyson Yerkes, a financier who had a major role in developing Chicago's mass transit system.

Northwest

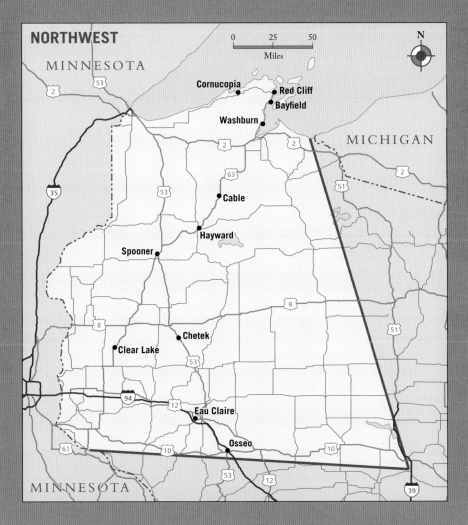

NORTHWEST

MINNESOTA

MICHIGAN

MINNESOTA

Cornucopia
Red Cliff
Bayfield
Washburn
Cable
Hayward
Spooner
Chetek
Clear Lake
Eau Claire
Osseo

0   25   50
Miles

N

The farther north you roam, the more elbow room. That's a good thing.

Seventy miles of Highway 13 are a National Scenic Byway that skirts along the southern shore of Lake Superior for a peaceful mix of water, vista, and farmland views. Look for roadside farm stands and rural art galleries, small towns with brawny charm, and no-nonsense boats built to haul home the catch of the day, day after day.

National forests and an overflow of pretty little lakes define the landscape. Trout fishing and whitewater canoeing bring nature lovers onto the Bois Brule River in Douglas County. Off the mainland in Bayfield County is Apostle Islands National Lakeshore. St. Croix National Scenic Riverway protects 250-some miles of waterways, including the fetching Namekagon River.

Look for slivers of sophistication to what feels rustic, be it in tiny-house lodging, gourmet pizzas on a farm, or nationally known musicians who show up for a tent show.

Bayfield

Population 584

Big Top Chautauqua

bigtop.org
(888) 244-8368

Your average musician sings of life's pitfalls, love found and lost, personal regrets, and maybe lessons learned. Rarer is the band whose original music becomes beloved because of its strong sense of place and attention to regional history.

Big Top Chautauqua's core performances are remarkable because of the setting, too. Homespun and multi-discipline shows occur under a canvas tent whose flaps roll up to let in fresh air whenever weather permits.

FAST FIVE

Apostle Islands Cruises provides narrated introductions to Apostle Islands National Lakeshore and its lighthouses. Most popular: the three-hour Grand Tour, which covers 55 miles. apostleisland.com, (800) 323-7619

Learn the chilling lore of shipwrecks, islands, and downtown buildings during a **Bayfield Ghost Walks** 2-hour walking tour. UFOs and a local Bigfoot figure into the tales. americanghostwalks.com, (833) 446-7813

Scenic areas are an inspiration for artists, and this community is no exception. To see much in one swoop, visit **Bayfield Artists' Guild**, whose multimedia gallery sells the works of dozens of local artists. bayfieldartistsguild.com, (715) 779-5781

Near the community are orchards, berry farms, and wineries—enough to be known as the **Fruit Loop**. Bayfield Apple Festival, in October, adds a parade and music to apple-centric menus.

Greunke's, in business since 1940 and eclectic because of memorabilia-filled walls, serves the local delicacy: whitefish livers. Big on breakfast and house-made pies, too. greunkesinn.com, (715) 779-5480

For more about Bayfield's charms: bayfield.org, (715) 779-3335.

"Multidiscipline" might mean a mix of music, poetry, storytelling, gentle humor, mild drama, and a slide show to illustrate lyrics as Blue Canvas Orchestra—the in-house band—works the stage.

Hundreds of nationally known artists, Arlo Guthrie to Ziggy Marley, have found these spotlights, too. The setting for performances is at the base of Mt. Ashwabay, a ski slope that overlooks Lake Superior.

Why a tent? It matches the unconventional, up-close vibe of Big Top Chautauqua. Why here? With musical commissions for a centennial celebration and a community jubilee in the 1980s came the demand for encores.

Warren Nelson gets credit for insisting on a tent for performances and creating more than a dozen of the unusual, free-spirited musicals (he and Betty Ferris were Big Top cofounders in 1986). When a philanthropist offered to secure a theater as home base, Nelson's pushback began for "culture under a tent," a tradition that began in 1874 with traveling performers and teachers at Lake Chautauqua, New York.

Bayfield's picturesque Chequamegon Bay already was attracting exceptional, transient musicians, despite the far-north location. "Some lived in cabins for $50 a month, back in the era of hootenannies," recalls Phillip Anich, a postmaster until becoming Big Top's first employee in 1989. "The music was presented at breakneck speed. It was jazz, blue-grass, folk," and a mix of other genres.

An audience of 900 fits under the canvas of blue and pearl gray ("Civil War colors," Phillip notes). Shows also stream as Tiny Tent Show episodes and air on public radio stations nationwide. The host is Michael Perry, a best-selling Wisconsin author with rural roots.

Most tasks for the nonprofit operation—car parking to venue cleanup—are executed by volunteers. Because the venue is unheated, the Big Top season is roughly June through September. Then some in-house musicians head back to teaching or other work; others take their show on the road to theaters and schools, where music doubles as a history lesson.

LODGING, HISTORIC AND NEW

An overnight at **Old Rittenhouse Inn** includes a hot made-to-order breakfast at the main building's gourmet restaurant, where the dinner menu has a fixed-price, five-course option. Specializing in the artful presentation of from-scratch cooking of soups to desserts. Rooms and suites are in a Queen Anne Victorian mansion and two historic  houses nearby. Open since 1973 and billed as Wisconsin's first bed-and-breakfast. rittenhouseinn.com, (715) 779-5111

New since 2021 is **Wild Rice Retreat**, a wellness center on 100 acres near Lake Superior and 1 mile south of Bayfield. Think yoga, writing, photography immersions, and private, guided, or group retreats. Lodging units—edgy Scandinavian design—sleep up to eight. Add trails to meander, a sauna house and rain room, retreat and dining buildings whose design complements  the woodsy setting. wildriceretreat.com, (715) 779-0178

When Phillip goes into a grade school, he is no longer surprised if students know the words to "Riding the Wind," a 1980s song about the area's beauty and ancestors. "It's so sing song-y—we're on our second generation" of those learning about their past as they sing.

Another early Nelson-Ferris tune remains a close-to-heart favorite for others who live close to Big Top Chautauqua's home. "I've sung it at so many funerals," says Phillip, who shares the chorus:

First, last and all the time
Here's where I wanna be
It's just a little town on the big lake
But it's home sweet home to me.

ON THE ISLAND

Worth a day trip or more is Madeline Island, the largest of the Apostle Islands at 14 miles long, 3 miles wide, and a 20-minute ferry ride from Bayfield.

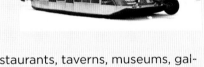

Bring a vehicle on **Madeline Island Ferry Line** or rent a bicycle or moped upon arrival. In winter, a passenger-only windsled keeps La Pointe and Bayfield connected if ice isn't thick enough for an ice road. madferry.com, (715) 747-2051

Near the dock and walkable are the restaurants, taverns, museums, galleries, and shops of **La Pointe**, population 428. Lodging is plentiful and diverse, including a horse farm.

A boardwalk connects **Big Bay** state and town parks; both have beaches and campsites. Fish, canoe, sail, or chill.

For more: madelineisland.com, (715) 747-2801.

Two fine arts programs earn acclaim far beyond the island and Midwest:

Madeline Island School of the Arts campus—for multiday workshops in painting, fiber arts, writing, photography—is a repurposed dairy farm. Additional school locations are in Santa Fe and Tucson. madelineartschool.com, (715) 747-2054

Madeline Island Chamber Music concerts showcase talented teen and young adult musicians in residence for intensive training. Students come from around the world, and the program works in partnership with MacPhail Center for Music. micm.org, (612) 321-0100

Cable

Population 177

American Birkebeiner

birkie.com
(715) 634-5025

No cross-country ski race in North America has larger participation than the annual American Birkebeiner. As many as 13,000 entrants from twenty-some countries ski up to 55 kilometers (about 34 miles) between the trailhead near Cable and downtown Hayward.

About one-half ski the premiere event. Others enter shorter events for classic and skate skiers, and thousands more show up just to watch it all.

All happens during five days in late February, weather permitting. Since the "Birkie" began with thirty-five skiers in 1973, the marquee race has only been canceled twice (2000, 2017) for lack of snow.

The event was inspired by skiers who helped an 18-month-old prince and his mother escape to safety during civil war in Norway in 1206. The rescuers were called *birkebeiner* skiers because they wore birch bark to protect their legs, and the rugged terrain they traversed was an inspiration for Norway's first Birkebeiner race in 1932.

OTHER FUN FEATS

Black Bear Inn, 10 miles north of Cable, on the third Saturday of February turns its backyard—surrounded by national forest—into a course for bar stool races as a snowmobile club fund-raiser. A max of sixty-four entrants attach skis to a bar stool, cross their fingers, and slide. "If you can sit on it and it will go down the hill, you can race it," rules state online, although it's more complicated than that. facebook.com/snojacks, (715) 739-6313

Chequamegon Mountain Bike Festival, in September, features off-road bicycling events of up to 40 miles. Limited to 3,100 racers, and the route includes part of the Birkie trail system; the Chequamegon Area Mountain Bike Association has marked and mapped 300-plus miles of off-road cycling trails. cheqmtb.com, cambatrails.org

IN THE NEIGHBORHOOD

The Rivers Eatery bakes breads and pizzas in a stone oven and sometimes hosts live music. Some pies are named after nearby rivers. That includes the Spirit Creek, with pulled pork, sauerkraut, and barbecue sauce. Look for the popular stop in a renovated warehouse that also is home to Redbery Books, which specializes in regional titles. theriverseatery.com, (715) 798-3123, (715) 798-5014

At **Cable Natural History Museum** is a wide array of taxidermy, a raptor center, and kid friendly nature exhibits. Local naturalists occasionally lead lectures and outings. cablemuseum.org, (715) 798-3890

Forest Library Lodge is the area's cozy public library, a 1920s log cabin that makes the National Register of Historic Places and one of 150 unusual properties featured in *The Public Library* by Robert Dawson (Princeton Architectural Press). forestlodgelibrary.org, (715) 798-3189

For more about the area: cable4fun.com, (800) 533-7454.

The baby? He returned to his homeland, was crowned King Haakon Haakonsson IV at age 13, and ruled Norway for 46 years.

Each year in Wisconsin, two skiers are selected to dress as the original birkebeiner "warriors," and a third poses as the prince's mother. They strap on wooden skis for the entire Birkie race course that takes them—and the ski racers—through forest, across a lake, and over American Birkebeiner International Bridge, to avoid Highway 63.

LOVELY LODGING

When I think about classic summer resort design in the Midwest, Old World architecture isn't the first thing to come to mind. That is a part of what makes **Garmisch Resort**, 8 miles east of Cable, unusual.

Among lodging options at the 65-acre property: the five-bedroom Edelweiss Haus and Blarney Castle, three-bedroom Alpine Haus, Schwaben Haus, and Chateau des Alpes.

Buildings live up to their names. Turrets, chalets, and gingerbread motifs mix with balconies, wood-carved sculptures, and wrap-around windows with expansive views of water and forest.

The Garmisch, in **Chequamegon National Forest**, has been a resort since 1904.

Inside the main, three-story lodge are a dining room and **Bierstube** cocktail lounge with heavy log beams and handcrafted woodwork. They are next to a roomy lounge for checkers, reading, and other rainy-day pursuits: A massive stone fireplace, cutouts of bears and fir trees, wood paneling, and assortment of taxidermy are about as Northwoods as it gets. garmischresort.com, (715) 794-2204

Just out the door is 3,200-acre Lake Namakagon, the national forest's biggest freshwater lake, and it is better suited for fishermen and nature lovers than sun worshippers and powerboat racers. Ducks, loons, heron, and osprey make their home here. So do bass, pike, walleye, and the fighting musky.

Also for your radar: **Lakewoods Resort and Lodge**, in the same family since 1906. The Lake Namakagon shoreline getaway has involved five generations, so far. A mural in the lounge illustrates the property's history.

The Lakewoods lodge burned in 1985 but was rebuilt, and the eighteen-hole Forest Ridges golf course was added in 1994. For rent are rooms, condos, and villas. lakewoodsresort.com, (715) 794-2561

Children as young as 6 years old will ski much shorter distances, individually and in teams. ParaBirkie racers use adaptive equipment during competition because of physical or visual impairments. Skiers in the Barkie Birkie are pulled along by a dog, which turns skiing into skijoring for up to 5 kilometers.

The overall 66.5-mile Birkie trail system is used all year by runners, hikers, and bikers. The nonprofit American Birkebeiner Ski Foundation organizes events all year to support active lifestyles.

Examples: In March is **Fat Bike Birkie** when mountain bikers compete on groomed trails. In September is **Birkie Trail Run Festival**, with runs of 1 to 100 kilometers for children to elite athletes.

Up next: Development of former Telemark Lodge property, near the trailhead, as Mt. Telemark Village, environmental conservancy and year-round trails, rec outlets and a fitness park for casual to elite athletes. Plus a basecamp with brewpub, coffeeshop, museum, and changing areas.

Also look for American Birkebeiner Ski Foundation to introduce a new professional cross-country ski team, Team Birkie.

Chetek

Population 2,172

Canoe Bay ESCAPE Village

escapevillages.com
(844) 696-3722

Dan Dobrowolski understands our growing curiosity to live large in a small space, and others are noticing his efforts from coast to coast.

The owner with his wife, Lisa, of remote Canoe Bay Resort—10 miles east of Chetek, and the Midwest's only Relais and Chateaux property—is a leader in the tiny-house movement. He has gained national attention for ESCAPE Homes, a venture that adds panache to RV living, cabin getaways, and second-home dreams.

The tiny-house movement encourages a downsizing of living space for the good of the environment and pocketbook. Eclectic designs for ESCAPE Homes start with the Vista BoHo at 187 square feet for under $50,000; compare that to 2,333 square feet for the median U.S. house sold in 2020.

Dan's 269-square-foot ESCAPE Traveler was one of twelve finalists in the Small Spaces that Live Large category of HGTV's 2015 Fresh Faces of Design contest. Dan and architect Kelly Davis have at least six basic models of tiny homes.

Often-standard amenities, furnishings, and ecologically friendly features in these houses wouldn't all make the cut in the average Northwoods cabin. Think solar power and standard kitchen appliances, radiant heat and flat-screen TV, on-demand hot water and flushing toilet with shower (maybe a tub, too). Add enough options—such as electric fireplace, dishwasher, spa tub, screened porch—and the price will hit six figures.

"We're using products that make a small carbon footprint and can be constructed to go entirely off the (energy) grid," Dan says. That's a reference to rooftop solar panels, a lithium battery, and more.

All-electric units are in demand and more earth-friendly than propane heat. Rainwater collection, composting or incinerating toilets, recycled products as insulation, and argon-filled windows are other energy-efficient possibilities.

FLASHBACK FLICKS

The Stardust, a two-screen drive-in theater, adds an old-school cool vibe northwest of Chetek. First-run films are shown seasonally and during fair weather, spring to fall. Bring your own lawn chairs and rent a radio to sit under the stars while taking in the scenery and double feature. Add a fish fry of bluegill or cod. stardustdriveinmovie.com, (715) 458-4587

Chetek calls itself "City of Lakes" because of the area's chain of six—Chetek, Moose Ear, Ojaski, Pokegame, Prairie, and Ten Mile—bodies of water. It's rich with wildlife and good for fishing bluegill to walleye. Lakeside resorts are plentiful. explorechetek.com, (715) 924-3200

LUXURY AT CANOE BAY

At the 300-acre and adults-only Canoe Bay Resort are twenty-seven suites and cottages, each designed for one couple. The resort is in rural Rusk County.

Miles of hiking trails meander into the woods, toward little Lost Lake. Kayaks and canoes skim 50-foot-deep Lake Wahdoon. Lodging units, designed by a student of Frank Lloyd Wright, are spaced far enough apart to ensure privacy.

Dan Dobrowolski's immigrant grandfather taught him how to fish on Canoe Bay's spring-fed lakes, how to navigate its forests of ash and oak, how to nourish a link between soul and land.

The grandparents farmed and raised nine children, including Dan's father, on 80 acres nearby. In the 1960s, a church bought lakeside acreage and turned it into a camp for two decades, then abandoned the effort.

Out came a "for sale" sign. Dan and his wife, Lisa, newlyweds living in Chicago, saw their chance to chase a dream and drastically change their lifestyle. They left careers in meteorology and journalism for stints as innkeepers of the highest degree.

"We're offering things that are real, not flashy, trendy, or appealing to a passing human interest," Lisa says. "We all tend to be overstimulated by work" and thrill-a-minute diversions. "This is about finding out what it's like when you don't have a schedule—being aware of what you hear, what you smell, and maybe taking a nap, just because you can."

Hundreds of book titles, many relatively new, fill shelves at the resort library. Dozens of movie and music DVDs also can be borrowed. Or maybe you'll be too busy looking for the perfect maple leaf during an autumn hike, then watching a couple of deer graze between cottage and lake.

"Having the leisure to let your best self come forward" is what Lisa hopes for her guests, who don't need to leave the property because the on-site chef offers three meals a day, often dipping into the bounty of the resort's robust garden, fenced to keep out wildlife. canoebay.com, (715) 924-4594

Big windows and cedar siding make ESCAPE models look like little Frank Lloyd Wright houses on wheels, and the Prairie style of design is deliberate. They resemble Canoe Bay Resort structures, which were the work of John Rattenbury, a protégé of the iconic architect.

"We had so much interest in our architecture at Canoe Bay," Dan explains. "These are very specific products, just like Canoe Bay, only on wheels."

An ESCAPE unit can be hitched and pulled, but weight might become an issue when hauling, so they are not meant for casual moving like a traditional RV. Construction occurs about 20 miles northwest of the tiny-house village, and they are sold factory direct.

"We're leading, not following" the tiny house movement, Dan believes. He says retirees to families with young children have expressed interest, and units are transported coast-to-coast. Dozens are rented through airbnb.com.

Dan recommends staying at a tiny house before investing in one. That is possible at ESCAPE Homes Village, tiny houses adjacent to Canoe Bay Resort that are available for overnight stays. Meals and access to Canoe Bay amenities are possible for an extra fee.

ESCAPE units have been sold to "all age groups and all types of people," Dan says. The pandemic was good for business because his tiny houses provided a safe vacation spot or new way to safely accommodate visitors.

Clear Lake

Population 1,099

Sawmill Pizza and Brew Shed

facebook.com/sawmillpizzabrewshed
weddingsinechovalley.com

The pizza farm is a phenomenon that surfaced in Wisconsin in the 1990s, and popularity shows no sign of dwindling. Farmers and other rural landowners use wood-fired ovens to quick-bake hundreds of pies for city slickers and others who appreciate, crave, or at least are curious about country life.

The point isn't to take the pizza and run home. It's to savor, linger, and notice how a change of setting can affect well-being for the better.

Dustin Booth and Emily Fradenburgh live on Polk County farmland with a former sawmill that his parents used to operate, near the end of a dead-end road in Echo Valley, 2 miles west of Clear Lake.

The couple converted their property into a haven for anybody in need of a quick break from stressful living, and a part of that work involves pizza.

Four days after Dustin and Emily married on their land in 2013, they began selling pizza from a wood-fired oven built inside the grain bin. Now they have two ovens and make up to 200 pies on Sunday Fundays, late May to early October, and book live music for the back porch of the pizza kitchen.

Two of four pizza selections change monthly. Exceptions are Pep Fest (pepperoni and co-jack cheese) and the most popular offering, Spicy Jameese (pepper and cheddar cheeses, strawberry jam, sriracha sauce).

Other unusual combos that gain raves: Expectant Mother (pickles, peanut butter, pepper cheese, pineapple); Dorcas Reilly (a green bean casserole pizza, named after the creator of the classic Thanksgiving

FAST FACT

The founder of Earth Day, U.S. Senator Gaylord Nelson, was born in Clear Lake in 1916 and buried there in 2005. The lifelong environmentalist was elected governor of Wisconsin in 1958. nelsonearthday.net

MORE FARMS

Note: Rules, offerings, and hours of business vary widely. On some farms are markets that sell fresh harvests.

A to Z Produce and Bakery—Pizza nights began in 1998, making the Pepin County farm a pioneer in the movement to bake and sell pies topped with close-to-home ingredients. atozproduceandbakery.com

Dancing Yarrow—Eat indoors or outside at the self-described "hippie farm" of 18 acres in Buffalo County. Lodging available: campsites, a rustic cabin, lodge rooms. Gluten-free and dairy-free pizzas are possible. farmtoforkretreat.com

The Stone Barn—Build your own pizza combo or trust the inventive blends of the Buffalo County hosts. The setting is lovely ruins of a century-old barn, in Norwegian Valley. thenelsonstonebarn.com

Stoney Acres—Brewing beer with organic hops and making pies with farm ingredients that include wheat for the crust. Eat in the heated beer hall if Marathon County weather is crummy. stoneyacres.farm

Suncrest Gardens—Book an overnight at the Buffalo County farmhouse, on 16 acres, after eating pizza and letting the kids burn energy on the playground. The motto: "our fields are our pantry." suncrestgardensfarm.com

Winghaven—The Trempealeau County farm's fourth and fifth generations lead the charge. Caramel apple dessert pizza? A fine match for the site's orchard history. winghavenpizzafarm.com

dish); and Bleu, Green, Eggs and Ham (blue cheese, asparagus, hard-boiled egg, Canadian bacon, cheddar, and black pepper).

In 2017, after Dustin learned to make beer, the Brew Shed opened. On tap are eight types of his beer. The most popular is Run of the Mill, a cream ale. Other favorites: Rubus Reamer Radler, a light ale with notes of raspberry and lemon; and Tipsy Bees, a nut brown with honey.

Guests bring whatever they need in addition to pizza and beer: snacks, desserts, no-alcohol beverages, yard games, picnic blankets. All are welcome to walk the acreage, which includes a 13-acre pond. Some come to spend the entire day.

In the proprietors' repertoire is a mix of practical and creative skills. They host weddings and also are known as Weddings in Echo Valley. Sometimes the sister businesses work together, providing a laid-back rehearsal dinner in addition to a dashing reception site.

"Every single Sunday, at least one couple visits—either they have been married here or their wedding is coming up," Emily says. Then they revisit for their anniversary or another event.

For the hosts, it's a dream come true because years ago they imagined a place where their guests could "eat, drink, and be married."

Cornucopia

Population 103

Apostle Islands National Lakeshore

nps.gov/apis
(715) 779-3397

Thanks to a "road closed" sign, my no-GPS-drive into town changed abruptly. First came farmland, then woods, while navigating from roads of concrete to dirt and gravel, sometimes under tree canopies dense enough to cast a solid blanket of shade during 15 puzzling miles.

I was barely north of Chequamegon-Nicolet National Forest, passing an occasional clearing and gravel pit but no cars or houses. Just as I began to wonder about wrong turns, sunlight reappeared, and I braked alongside a guy in a parked truck, cell phone at his ear.

"Where's Cornucopia?" I asked, and he seemed amused. "This is it," he reassured. "You made 'er all right."

PURE MUSH

Hit the hills of Bayfield Peninsula with **Wolfsong Adventures in Mushing**, 10 miles east of Cornucopia, where an introduction to dog sledding lasts up to 4 hours. Learn to harness and drive a team or let someone else do the navigating. Most of the working dogs are Seppala Siberians. wolfsongadventures.com, (715) 209-4551

The rugged community near the peak of Wisconsin, on the shore of Lake Superior, was nicknamed "Corny" more than a century ago. I've seen old-time photos of women dressing herring in the 1950s, when tons of the fish were harvested daily. Others showed sleighs pulling lumber in winter; a dozen lumbering camps used to operate in the area.

Some of that continues, but people also come to Cornucopia to discover Apostle Islands National Lakeshore. The National Park Service property—a twenty-one-island archipelago and 12 miles of shoreline—is pure wilderness with dramatic scenery. Wind-whipped and wave-lashed sandscapes form cliffs and sea caves of red sandstone.

These grand sculptures of nature—delicate archways, hidden passageways, steep swoops, and vaulted ceilings—won't look the same from day to day. Lighting, weather, season, and mood of the tempestuous Great Lake all influence what is seen.

The islands are a birder's delight—home to loons, bald eagles, gulls, and cormorants. The most popular day trip is a 1-mile paddle along the Lake Superior shore, starting at Meyers Beach (4 miles northeast of Cornucopia), to reach sea caves that extend 2 more miles.

"So that's a 5- or 6-mile paddle," says Neil Howk, retired National Park Service ranger. The journey typically takes 3 or 4 hours, "but if the wind picks up, that's it. You're done for the day—all your plans can go out the window."

Guided day trips by local outfitters follow the shoreline route and include time for a beachside lunch. They involve sea kayaks, which are bigger and more stable than the average kayak. How close paddlers get to sea caves depends upon luck, skills, and fortitude.

Freak waves can come and go in minutes. The Great Lakes contain riptides, just as oceans do. An experienced paddler might be a thrill-seeker who welcomes the challenge of confronting 4-foot-high waves—or be spooked by surges one-half that height.

Rustic camping, by reservation only, is allowed on eighteen of the Apostle Islands and one mainland site. Some campers arrive by water

IN THE NEIGHBORHOOD

The Friday fish fry is a beloved Wisconsin tradition, and that might mean all-you-can-eat herring, whitefish, and trout at **The Fat Radish**, a farm-to-table restaurant where the fresh catch of the day is truly local, and from-scratch fare with gourmet flair is business as usual.

Just down the road is family-owned **Halvorson Fisheries**, which has worked the lake for about one-half century. Look for the harbor shop where fresh-as-it-gets and smoked fish are sold. thefatradish.weebly.com, (715) 742-3200; on Facebook, (715) 742-3402

Near Halvorson's are weathered vessels and other relics of commercial fishing heritage; open part time from mid-June to Labor Day is **Green Shed Museum**, a long-ago fish house with outdoor tables for harborside picnicking. cornucopiawisconsin.pastperfectonline.com

Also along the harbor, in converted fishing shacks, are shops that sell fine art to farm products. Downtown is **Ehlers**, a general store since 1915, selling an unpredictable mix of food, hardware, souvenirs, and locally made merchandise. Spend the night in simple spaces where fashionable décor is not a priority or find your way to Northwoods-elegant **Siskiwit Bay Lodge**, a bed-and-breakfast with accommodations that face Lake Superior. siskiwit baylodge.com, (715) 742-3900

An annual fish fry in July feeds hundreds of people, and lots of the locals help make it happen. One fund-raiser might help the volunteer fire department. Another might restore a historic fishing boat or buy a new flagpole in the cemetery.

Corny is wild enough for the occasional timber wolf or black bear to wander into town. Much of the area's appeal rests in the delight of discovering what—for now—isn't aggressively advertised. If you need help doing that, just ask around. Hint: pack an empty milk jug or two, for artesian drinking water from a public beach well. visitcornucopia.com taxi; others are experienced kayakers who carry weather radios and expect to adjust plans on short notice.

"Lake Superior is not the place to go to learn to sea kayak for a multiple-day trip," Neil says. "Conditions can get very rough—big waves, mainly—and these islands are scattered over (hundreds of) square miles, with at least 2 or 3 miles between islands."

National Park Service staff search for overdue or missing kayakers several times a year. Even in 90-degree weather, kayakers should pack wetsuits in overnight gear because water temperature hovers around 60 degrees.

In winter, wind and ice turn sea caves into another kind of beautiful but at-your-own-risk proposition. Gusts whisk away snow cover, leaving slick patches of ice. Surfaces turn uneven, and ice thickness varies, as do the size of ice cracks.

Expect to walk a mile on the lake before reaching the sea caves. Then walk another mile or two, to find surreal configurations of icicles and crystals on cliffs and sandstone caverns. Allow at least 3 hours for the adventure and be sure to return before sunset.

Rangers aren't always around to help, no one leads guided tours, and no shuttles travel to the ice caves. Don't expect cell phone reception or toilets.

Until ice is at least 8 inches thick along the entire route, the NPS does not recommend ice cave visits. Sometimes no ice cave visits are advised for an entire winter, because of precarious conditions. Call the park office for daily updates.

Hayward

Population 2,533

Lumberjack World Championships

lumberjackworldchampionships.com
(715) 634-2484

High levels of speed and physical risk separate extreme sports—such as mountain biking and skateboarding—from other feats of athleticism. In Hayward, perilous tests of skill are all about burly heritage.

Lumberjacks have chopped and sawed competitively in Hayward since the 1890s, when the community and Namekagon River that

runs through it were the hub for logging an abundance of white pine. Friendly challenges arose during downtime in lumber camps.

Since 1960, Lumberjack World Championships are a more organized test of prowess in timber sports. Men and women from as far as Australia and New Zealand compete at the riverside Lumberjack Bowl, where world records are meant to be broken in eighteen categories.

Founder Tony Wise, who died in 1995, aimed to help outsiders discover Hayward and, as he described it, "perpetuate and glorify the working skills of the American lumberjack." More than one hundred athletes compete, teens to older adults.

"Olympics of the Forest" is a nickname for the spectacle of log-rolling and ax throwing. Speed climbers scale a cedar pole of 60 or 90

WORTHY DETOUR

A mom and her two daughters co-own and operate **Northstar Homestead Farm** and **Farmstead Creamery**, 20 miles east of Hayward. Behind the farmers' "live life with a purpose" mantra are workshops (such as weaving, felting), a gift shop (wearable art, gift boxes), specialty grocer (farm veggies, meats), and to-go treats made with farm ingredients, including bakery and gelato (made with sheep's milk).

Events have included pizza nights (made in a stone oven outdoors) and multicourse group meals. The setting: a century-old farm with aquaponics greenhouse and deep commitment to environmental sustainability. northstarhomestead.com, (715) 462-3453

THE MUSKY FACTOR

The official state fish of Wisconsin since 1955 is the muskellunge, a strong and large fighter. Biggest summer event in Hayward is **Musky Fest**, in June; look for fish-themed arts/crafts, carnival rides, car show, and parade with Musky Queen royalty. Live music and contests (cornhole, fun runs, hula hooping, melon eating) are plentiful. muskyfest.com

Most unusual in Hayward is a replica of the "musky" that is 143 feet long, 40 feet tall, and anchoring the **Fresh Water Fishing Hall of Fame and Museum**. Walk into the gut and toothful mouth of the concrete/steel/fiberglass fish (ending with an outdoor observation platform). In addition to fishing artifacts, the museum documents world-record catches for each of the nation's freshwater species. freshwater-fishing.org, (715) 634-4440

A world-record musky in 1949 (67 pounds, 8 ounces) is one of many wall mounts at the downtown **Moccasin Bar**, big on odd taxidermy displayed under glass. For example: boxing raccoons, other critters gambling, a quartet on hind legs that hold little beer mugs and look ready to sing. Each is a remarkable, detailed diorama that has lasted decades. (715) 634-4211

At **West's Hayward Dairy**, in business since the 1950s, a signature flavor is Chunky Musky: banana ice cream, walnuts, dark chocolate. The forty flavors usually offered daily will include some that rotate seasonally. westsdairy.com, (715) 634-2244

Angry Minnow Brewing Pub, in a repurposed 1889 lumber company headquarters, makes cheese-stuffed pretzels with spent grain. Add a bowl of soup or stick to whatever is on tap, be it River Pig Pale Ale or Big Brook IPA. angryminnow.com, (715) 934-3055

Treeland, a Hayward resort that began as a fishing camp in 1928, hosts the annual **Lake Chippewa Flowage Musky Hunt** in September and **Musky Fly Fishing Championship** in October. treelandresorts.com, (715) 462-3874

feet in height. Boom runs, a two-person test of balance, are a careful and head-to-head sprint along the length of two logs in water, ends chained together.

Solo competitors and teams of two use a bucking saw to manually cut through a white pine log of up to 20 inches in diameter. Using a "hot saw"—single-motor power saw—to make three vertical cuts through a log is a one-man race of strength and deftness against time.

Music, vendors, 5-kilometer Lumberjack Run, and "swinging ax beer garden" are part of the weekend, too.

Although the world championships are three days in late June, outdoor **Fred Scheers Lumberjack Shows** are a summerlong tradition in Hayward (and Minocqua, population 411). World champs and others compete during 90-minute, family-friendly shows that are tempered with comedy skits and logging history lessons.

Shows are named after a native son and successful real estate investor who was a teen when winning the first of four world championships in logrolling. scheerslumberjackshow.com, (715) 634-6923

Osseo

Population 1,811

Norske Nook

norskenook.com
(715) 597-3069

No professional pie maker in Wisconsin wins more national championships than Norske Nook, which began as farm wife Helen Myhre's little café in 1973. To say her pies are good is an understatement.

Those pies are what transformed Norske Nook into a tourist stop and media darling. Pie-in-mouth satisfaction increased word-of-mouth advertising nationwide. Count former President Clinton and musician Randy Travis among those who have sought a slice from Norske Nook, also known for authentic Norwegian meals.

The bakery-restaurant amassed forty-seven blue ribbons from American Pie Council competition before the pandemic suspended the annual event. Each year, hundreds of entries from bakers in three divisions (commercial, independent, amateur) were rated by appearance, taste, aftertaste, mouth feel, and crust quality (texture, flavor, flakiness). Entries were divided into dozens of flavor categories.

As one of roughly seventy-five judges a few years ago, my answer to the last question for each entry—Do you want more of this pie?—wasn't an automatic "yes," especially as exceptional bakers raised expectations and appetite dwindled. Dozens of whole pies, then slices, appeared and disappeared in apple-pie order.

All was a serious endeavor: no sipping coffee with pie (it masks flavor). No talking about a pie when it is presented. Sample the crust twice, at the front and back of each slice. Mask facial reactions. Work independently within your subset of judges.

I mention this to drive home the point that all those Norske Nook blue ribbons were not easy wins. Neither would they make anyone rich. Contestants paid to enter and invested in lodging with a reliable oven to expertly prepare entries. Their quest was modest, monetarily: a $200 blue ribbon (or the $5,000 Best of Show prize). The value of bragging rights? Huge.

Banana cream, blueberry, and peach pies from Norske Nook bakers have dominated traditional contest categories. Bakers also excel at using cream cheese as a key ingredient, earning seven blues for adding lemon, apples, blueberries, pecans, pumpkin, raspberries, strawberries.

Still other prize winners have unusual flavor profiles: Banana Toffee, Blueberry Lemonaid, Butterfinger, Coconut Pineapple Dream, Maple Raisin, Pecan Stout, Raspberry Peach Melba, Snickers Caramel.

What baking secret applies to all? There's no skimping on fillings. A berry pie might weigh 8 pounds. Meringues are lofty—several inches high. New recipes were tested and retested until the owner and

CHEESE, PLEASE

Forty-five miles northeast of Osseo is Marieke Gouda, whose cheeses win international awards. That's not unusual in Wisconsin, but at this destination—Thorp, population 1,795—you can watch the cows proceed through the milking parlor and stay for lunch at Café DUTCHess, where farmstead cheeses enrich pancakes to quesadillas. Guided tours scheduled during summer. mariekegouda.com, (715) 669-5230

his regional manager (Jerry Bechard and Cindee Borton-Parker, for decades) agreed they were ready to debut.

Nationwide media attention (including Helen's appearance on a David Letterman talk show, to make sour cream raisin pie) heightened cravings for a taste of Norske Nook. The wait for seating kept growing, so a much larger bakery and restaurant were built. It is across the street from the original café, which turned into a Scandinavian gift shop and coffeehouse.

For sale in the gift shop: fruit pie fillings by the jar, hardwood rolling pins, rosemaling, and more.

Then Norske Nooks opened in Rice Lake (population 9,040) and DeForest (population 10,811), but even with these bigger locations, the

WORTHY DETOURS

To the north: Cadott, population 1,498, brings in nationally known acts for multiday music festivals on 360 acres that include 7,000 camp-sites. Founders call it the largest campground in Wisconsin. A shuttle links the grounds to other lodging. Fifty bands per festival perform on a main stage with natural amphitheater and four side stages. **Country Fest** (in June) and **Rock Fest** (in July) began in the 1990s; tickets go on sale several months ahead. countryfest.com, rock-fest.com, (800) 326-3378

To the south: Wisconsin is not known for robust blueberry production, but an excellent microclimate at **Cain's Orchard** makes it possible to grow ten varieties. Bring buckets to pick the berries when the second-generation owners of the family business decide the time is ripe. The farm is near Hixton, population 456. cainsorchard.com, (715) 963-2052

To the east: Camp or stay in a rustic cabin, modern hermitage, or guesthouse room at the **Christine Center**, a spirituality retreat. It is near Willard, population 525, and Amish farms. Optional add-on: buffet-style meals, most vegetarian. Make the trip for independent, guided, or group program retreats (delving into yoga, meditation, grief, healing, compassionate connections). Or volunteer time in exchange for lodging, meals, and access to facilities. Expect earth-friendly practices: composting, solar panels, geothermal heating. christinecenter.org, (715) 267-7507

To the west: **Together Farms** is near Mondovi, population 2,845, and hosts Burger Nights, accompanied by area musicians, May through October. Burgers are made with beef, lamb, and pork from livestock raised at the farm. Add craft beers, sodas. A farm shop sells meats, meal kits, soaps, balms. togetherfarms.com, (715) 210-4740

Osseo location stays busy. Fans know it's the nucleus of the business, and it's convenient—a quick scoot off of Interstate 94.

At the end of 2021, Jerry retired and sold the Norske Nooks to managers Kaye Rhody and Stacy Campbell. Both women were hired as Norske Nook dishwashers and worked their way up.

Stacy is among the bakers who help develop new pie recipes that turn into award winners. Kim Hanson, another longtime employee, makes sure pies and other foods stay consistent among all Norske Nook locations.

What else makes the menu special? Scandinavian meatballs, thin pancakes with lingonberries, and the option of tortilla-like *lefse* as a wrap for breakfast sandwiches and dinner. Think of it as a Norwegian enchilada: lefse with a filling of eggs, hash browns, and cheese, then topped with hollandaise. Or lefse around hot beef and mashed potatoes, topped with gravy.

The popular lutefisk and meatball dinner, on the first Sunday of December, traditionally starts with pickled herring and ends with *rømmergrøt* pudding and a rosette pastry or *sandbakkel* cookie.

Red Cliff

Population 1,313

Frog Bay Tribal National Park

redcliff-nsn.gov/frogbay
(715) 779-3750

Frog Bay Tribal National Park is not the kind of place that will gain praise for its size, dramatic features, amenities, or attendance. The opening of this first national tribal park, in far-north Wisconsin, occurred with little public fanfare during the summer of 2012.

Signage remains modest. You might not know how to get there unless

instructed. You might not, with a casual glance, realize the land's signifi-cance. The parking lot is small, and the route ends with a dirt-sand road. Park boundaries seem unclear.

These 175 acres include undeveloped Lake Superior shoreline. Don't expect lifeguards, boat docks, or floating rafts for swimmers. The lake-shore view speaks quietly but profoundly for itself.

"The intent is to keep it pristine," explained Ellen Kwiatkowski, while executive director of Bayfield Regional Conservancy. "It's meant to be silent and rustic." The Red Cliff Band of Lake Superior Chippewa are stewards of the property; the tribal nation's name is a nod to terrain near the Great Lake they know as Gichigami (various spellings).

Two park trails, each less than a half mile, end at the sandy shore with views of Apostle Islands National Lakeshore. More difficult is the 1-mile Ravine Trail that goes up, over, and through unlogged boreal forest.

The park and another 125 acres under conservation management protect sensitive ecological habitats. Globally endangered plants and

EVERGLADES OF THE NORTH

Forty miles south of Red Cliff is another far-north tribal nation, Bad River Ojibwe, whose reservation con-tains the biggest natural wild rice beds of the Great Lakes. These **Kakagon and Bad River Sloughs** are a National Natural Landmark and a Ramsar Site (Wetland of International Importance). Canada lynx and piping plover shore-birds, endangered species, are among the wildlife at home there.

Human access to the swampy area, nicknamed "Everglades of the North," is limited to Bad River members and the tribe's natural resources staff. More than 90 percent of the nation's 125,000 acres are wetlands along 38 miles of Lake Superior shore and nearly 500 miles of streams.

The August Bad River Manoomin Powwow celebrates the annual wild rice harvest, which is done by hand and during a designated, regulated season. Tribal courts prohibit the use of machinery or motorized boat during harvest. badriver-nsn.gov, (715) 682-7111

IN THE NEIGHBORHOOD

Four miles south of Frog Bay is **Legendary Waters Resort and Casino**, which faces Lake Superior. All forty-seven guest rooms and suites have a water view. An option to resort lodging is the adjacent RV and tent park. The marina is a popular launch point for kayaks.

In the casino are 240 slot machines, blackjack and poker tables, and seasonal tournaments (including cribbage, bingo). A birchbark canoe made by Marvin DeFoe of the Red Cliff hangs as art. In display cases are Chippewa photos and artifacts. legendarywaters.com, (800) 226-8478

Tall pines surround **Copper Crow Distillery**, the country's first distillery owned by a Native American on a reservation. "Like a crow, we wondered about our purpose," founders Curt and Linda Basina acknowledge online. They are members of the Red Cliff and were high school sweethearts.

Whey, a waste product in cheesemaking, adds a bit of sweetness and deepens the flavor profile of gin and vodka. University of Wisconsin Stout helped the distiller experiment with this unusual-for-spirits ingredient. Seasonal craft cocktails are served in the tasting room, where wood tables were made with repurposed bowling lanes. coppercrowdistillery.com, (715) 779-0275

ninety-some species of birds have been identified in the forest, wetlands, and Frog Bay estuary. Bobcats, black bears, and wolves have been sighted. Part of the area is open only to tribal members for specific uses such as the harvest of wild rice by hand.

"Protecting the site will also help preserve tribal cultural traditions and way of life," states the U.S. Coastal and Estuarine Land Conservation Program, which assisted the Red Cliff with land acquisition and management.

The land "was used for many generations as a teaching ground for plant medicine, a place for sitting out (fasting), and as a beautiful, scenic area for canoeing," notes the Great Lakes Indian Fish and Wildlife Commission.

The Red Cliff reservation of 14,093 acres is 1 mile wide, 14 miles long, and among the smallest tribal reservations in Wisconsin.

As Richard LaFernier of the Red Cliff led the way to Frog Bay's shore, he sampled wild raspberries, pointed out poisonous snakeberries, and recalled his boyhood of sledding on ravines and canoeing from bay to islands. The moss that we walked on, amid the tall cedars and pines, felt like a thick and spongy carpet.

Twice he found a feather on the beach. Twice he carefully smoothed and stuck the quill upright on the sand. "We don't let the feather touch the ground, out of respect for the bird," he explains.

"This land was never mine to own," he adds. "It belongs to the Creator, but I would protect it."

Spooner

Population 2,477

Wisconsin Great Northern Railroad

spoonertrainride.com
(715) 635-3200

Locomotive whistles were a once-common part of Spooner, which at its peak saw eighteen daily passenger trains, eleven logging trains, ten freight trains, four section crews, and fifty-five chain gang crews.

The city was a divisional headquarters for rail lines by the late 1800s, employing 600 to cover all aspects of railroad operations: agents to engineers, conductors to dispatchers, brakemen to repairmen.

What a perfectly logical location for train rides and restoration today. Spooner's passenger service ended in 1961, but Wisconsin Great Northern Railroad excursions relive the nostalgia and slow the pace of travel.

Restored railroad cars meander through countryside

for fall color tours, visits with Santa, meals of pizza (made onboard), and multicourse dinners. The Sky Parlour lounge car from the Santa Fe El Capitan (known for its Chicago–Los Angeles circuit) is used for wine and cheese excursions.

Woods, fields, and rivers are what customers see while heading north toward Springbrook, population 89. The route follows the Namekagon River and takes a trestle bridge over Bean Brook.

Boarding is five miles north of Spooner; a depot and railyard were built in the middle of a hay field in 2013. Before that, trips began at the once-grand depot in downtown Spooner.

Owners Greg and Mardell Vreeland began as a two-person operation. Now they have twenty full-time employees. Under their care are forty passenger cars and fifteen locomotives; about half were rebuilt. They average a couple of new acquisitions per year and are working to upgrade car interiors.

Trains are a lifelong love for Greg, who met Mardell in 1992, and two years later bought their first car to restore. Their business began in 1997, and the couple rebuilt a chapel car so they could get married in it in 2004. Son Alexander, born six years later, already is a railroad operator in training.

Greg knows that he has "a lifetime of work" but seems exceptionally excited by his recent acquisition of the 1935 Mark Twain Zephyr, a lighter, faster, and streamlined design during its heyday. Cars were

IN THE NEIGHBORHOOD

Wisconsin Canoe Heritage Museum preserves some of the more historically significant vessels to navigate North America's rivers and lakes. Dugout, birchbark, and canvas canoes document the boat's evolution and diversity. Filling this revamped 1912 feed mill are canoes considered significant in design, workmanship, and quality. wisconsincanoeheritagemuseum.org, (715) 635-5002

The world's largest hatchery for Wisconsin's state fish, the muskellunge, is named after former Governor Tommy Thompson and in Spooner. The **Fish Hatchery** produces a majority of the musky and walleye that the state stocks. Learn more at the visitor center. dnr.wisconsin.gov, (715) 635-4147

The nonprofit **Arts in Hand** sells the creative works of at least forty regional artists; a few occasionally demonstrate their craft or offer classes. The setting is a repurposed 1904 bank. Look for a map that pinpoints dozens of other artist studios and galleries in northwest Wisconsin. artsinhand.com, (715) 635-9303

In a 1915 building and former hardware store lives **Northwind Book and Fiber**, whose merchandise reflects the owners' passions. Besides yarns and best sellers, that means fine chocolates and artist-made jewelry. northwindbook.com, (715) 635 6811

Go glamping at **Namekagon Waters Retreat**, a little-advertised yurt on 40 acres that comfortably sleeps up to four. Equipped with homey furnishings and electricity. Water is carried in, and a tidy outhouse is a few steps outside. Relax in the sauna, book a massage, walk the outdoor labyrinth. Near the Namekagon River and trails for hiking, cross-country skiing. (715) 520-7641

Spooner Rodeo, a tradition since the 1950s, attracts professional cowboys and cowgirls from around the country to compete in nationally sanctioned events in July. On the docket: barrel racing, bareback riding, bull riding, steer wrestling, roping, and mutton bustin'. Lots of horses high-step it in the rodeo parade. spoonerrodeo.com, (715) 635-9696

For more about Spooner, so proud of historic preservation that it offers a self-guided tour of tin ceilings, and the area's other small towns: washburncounty.org.

named after Twain's most beloved characters (Becky Thatcher, Huck Finn, Tom Sawyer, Injun Joe).

"We are specializing in operations that are unique," Greg explains. "We have the only moving bed-and-breakfast train in the country" and "the only dinner train with all-private-compartment seating." When renovation is finished, he will add the world's only operating stainless-steel, shovel-nose Zephyr train.

Trip lengths vary, 90 minutes to overnight. A bed-and-breakfast booking includes accommodations for two, private bathroom, dinner, and breakfast. The train returns to the station at 8 p.m. and parks; the cocktail lounge stays open a while longer.

What else? Friends of **Spooner Railroad Park** aim to educate others about local railroad history through educational signage and restoration of railroad facilities that include a weigh station, roundhouse, and 90-foot turntable that are owned by the city. The ongoing project turns a blighted area into a public park and event space. spoonerrailroadpark.org, (715) 416-4622

Tour guides include retired railroaders at **Railroad Memories Museum**, in a 1902 railroad depot. Full of artifacts and memorabilia: railroad bells and whistles to vintage art and advertising. Open late May to early September. On Facebook, (715) 635-3325

Washburn

Population 2,051

Chequamegon Books

chequamegonbooks.com
(715) 373-2899

Richard Avol is one part scholar, one part sleuth, and one part book appraiser whose business would be far less surprising in a major U.S. college town than a faraway hamlet.

He and his wife, Carol, in 1995 sold their bookstore in Madison and moved to Northwoods Wisconsin with 1,300 boxes of unprocessed books from storage and the will to succeed in very different surroundings. That was before e-commerce was commonplace.

They had visited the Chequamegon Bay area in all seasons and were drawn by the lower cost of doing business and growing number of friends who moved there.

"This area is a small enclave of artists, thinkers, back-to-the-land, old hippies, retirees, locals, progressives, people who had successful careers elsewhere (mainly Minneapolis) and decided they wanted to do something else with the rest of their lives," Richard says.

The Avols' Chequamegon Books, a three-person operation with assistant Britton Doolittle, goes beyond the generic bookstore's stock of best sellers. Within the new and used titles is much obscure content, rare books, first editions, and signed copies. More than 34,000 books are listed for sale online; most work time is spent processing orders.

Richard's half-joking motto is, "We have books others don't have or wouldn't even want to have." The ongoing bet is that enough scholars and others will seek the unusual inventory. "Don't get me wrong—we are not just some strange bookstore in a remote place. We do have books for almost everyone," although romance novels, "supermarket-type books," and pornography are not stocked.

He is especially proud of the store's large and curated collection of Native American books. Varied and high-quality art and music sections are "a holdover from our Madison days." Science/physical science titles "are what really set us apart from most other bookstores."

FAST FACT

Admission is free to **Northern Great Lakes Visitor Center**, 8 miles south of Washburn, where exhibits and murals turn back time, movies introduce area wildlife and Native American culture. Nature trails pass marsh and meadow. nglvc.org, (715) 685-9983

FAN FAVORITES

Treat yourself to chocolate *babka,* fruit-filled *kolaches,* or cashew-cranberry granola from **Café CoCo**, serving breakfast and lunch, too. Most unusual: ostrich ears—flat, crispy, and frosted cinnamon rolls. coconorth.com, (715) 373-2253

Patsy's Bar and Grill, a tavern with upstairs brothel in the 1800s, is best known for burgers, deemed best in Bayfield County. Friday fish fry features whitefish from Lake Superior. patsysbarandgrill.com, (715) 373-5792

Nut Brown Ale from **South Shore Brewery and Taphouse** earned a World Beer Cup silver medal. It was the craft brewer's first beer and is served all year. Also in the portfolio of nearly four dozen seasonal taps: Anniversary Ale (extra special bitter) and Willie's Alloa (scotch ale). southshorebrewery.com, (715) 682-9199

Just north of town is **Good Thyme**, a caterer with dinner restaurant in a century-old house with wrap-around porch on 5 acres. Serving pizzas, entrées with unconventional twists. goodthyme.catering, (715) 373-5255

The Avols began buying overstock and remainder books while in Madison but dealt with small, esoteric wholesalers, to better compete with national bookstore chains.

"For example, we stocked a lot of higher-end art, photography, and architecture books. These were beautiful books from great publishers but only available in very small quantities. Our store became known for having these and many other high-quality, scholarly books in all fields."

What is not stocked can be searched because Richard long ago established relationships with bookseller associations around the world. Setting prices for unusual or limited-availability books "takes a lot of research to determine what we have and who may want them," but it is work that Richard enjoys.

"As a serious bookseller, you must be very inquisitive," he says. "And as a former hoped-to-be college professor, studying and learning are things I like to do." He and Carol do appraisals of private collections, too.

"I knew early on that the key to this type of bookselling (used books) was buying the right books for what your store wanted to be," Richard says.

The setting is a historic brownstone with cozy areas for lingering. Little nonbook merchandise is for sale. "On occasion, we have an odd antique or other item that we found and thought interesting," Richard

WORTHY DETOUR

Forty miles west is the emerging **Oulu Cultural and Heritage Center**, where guided tours include renovated historic buildings: homesteads as old as 1899, an old-time Finnish sauna, schoolhouse, and dairy cooperative. Oulu, town population 560, is named after a city in Finland, and about three-fourths of the town's first homesteaders were Finnish immigrants; many still claim Finnish ancestry. ouluculturalcenter.org, (715) 372-4849

Jalapeños are slipped into grilled cheese sandwiches and crepe-like pancakes at **Delta Diner**, a shiny and rehabbed Silk City diner built in 1940. Surrounded by Chequamegon-Nicolet National Forest and the biggest draw to Delta, population 273. Sister businesses are the seasonal **Taste Budz**, for coffees and ice cream, and **TapShack**, for jerk chicken and meats. deltadiner.com, (715) 372-6666

Pick up a bottle of mead from the first place in Wisconsin to make and sell it commercially: **White Winter Winery**, Iron River, population 637. Crafting hard ciders and spirits, too, using fruits and honey harvested locally. Some products are international award winners. whitewinter.com, (715) 372-5656

acknowledges. "When buying books, you run into other things, but unlike many other stores, we have no sidelines."

He considers his work to seek, find, and sell quality books a life mission or calling. "We sometimes think—perhaps conceitedly—of ourselves as one of the last bastions of culture, civilization, knowledge, and happiness. We know we do not appeal to all, not even close to the majority of people."

Northeast

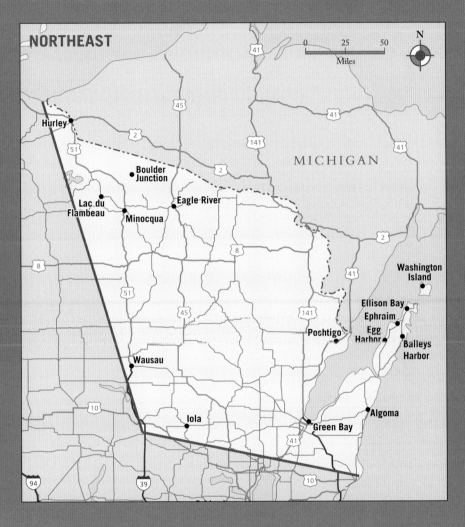

0   25   50
Miles

N

MICHIGAN

Hurley

Boulder
Junction

Lac du
Flambeau

Eagle River

Minocqua

Washington
Island

Ellison Bay
Ephraim
Egg
Harbor

Balleys
Harbor

Pochtigo

Wausau

Iola

Algoma

Green Bay

Welcome to an exquisite study in contrasts.

Follow highways 42 and 57 through the bountiful Door County peninsula. The 66-mile loop is a National Scenic Byway that shows why we love to drift north during all seasons.

Outlining the "Door" are 300 miles of shoreline and eleven historic lighthouses, one of the largest U.S. concentrations per county. Within those parameters are five state parks, nineteen county parks, numerous smaller parks, and nature preserves.

Our precious playground, where farmers' favored fruit is the Montmorency cherry, is in northern Wisconsin but not truly Up North in spirit: that distinction is reserved for far more remote acreage and burgs.

Most northern Wisconsin counties have fewer than 20,000 residents. Scarce is the four-lane highway, and two-lane roads may or may not be paved. Think wild, rugged, and simply gorgeous landscapes.

Chequamegon-Nicolet National Forest takes the lead in much of what is admired or done for fun in the Northwoods. Fishing reels in tourists, too, but consider hiring a guide to decide where to cast a line. A multitude of choices await.

Algoma

Population 3,243

von Stiehl Winery

vonstiehl.com
(920) 487-5208

In an 1868 Italianate building, one block from Lake Michigan, the oldest licensed winery in Wisconsin began business in 1967. The vintner was a local doctor, Charles Stiehl, who began making cherry wine as a hobby.

Until the good doctor asked for a license, state government had no method in place to regulate wine production. His brick building in downtown Algoma, where wine is served and stored, had divergent uses before this one: brewery, netting company, factory, and feed storage. Modern-day production happens in a newer building, across the street.

Underground is wine barrel aging in limestone tunnels from the Civil War era. Upstairs is a cozy lounge for wine lovers to dawdle with a Naughty Girl or Sassy Sangria, two of von Stiehl's popular reds. For sampling in the tasting room are at least forty wine varietals.

Stiehl's original recipes for sweet cherry and dry cherry wines, the foundation for the company, continue to be bottled. The fruit? Montmorency cherries grown in Door County. Juices for other fruit wines come from New York, Michigan, and elsewhere in Wisconsin.

Grapes are sourced from California and Washington to supplement what is grown at the winemaker's vineyard, 6 miles away. An exception is sweet Crimson Royale, made with New York concord grapes.

Four decades after business began, von Stiehl came up with a nostalgic tonic label and introduced Doc Stiehl's Cherry Bounce, in honor of the founder. The elixir, which blends cherry brandy with Doc's original

IN THE NEIGHBORHOOD

The **National Shrine of Our Lady of Good Help**, 15 miles west of Algoma, welcomes the faithful and curious from throughout the world. The sacred space, since 1871, is the only Vatican-acknowledged location of Virgin Mary sightings in the United States.

Take a self-guided tour of the grounds, grottoes, and chapel, which are between farm fields in Brown County. championshrine.org, (920) 866-2571

FAST FIVE

In 2013, von Stiehl opened **Ahnapee Brewery** in a garage that turned into a taproom. The business was sold in 2020 to the brewmaster, who moved the business a few doors down the street. Pints and growlers are filled with beer made in small batches. Little Soldier, an amber ale, honors the Civil War veteran who brewed beer when Algoma was called "Ahnapee." ahnapeebrewery.com, (920) 785-0822

Shop for a wedding gown, prom dress, pageant outfit, or quinceañera attire at jam-packed **Tina Marie's**, a boutique of unique and customized clothing, especially for women and special occasions. Doesn't matter if you need a fancy hat for the Kentucky Derby or a tiara for a parade float. tinamariesboutique.com, (920) 487-3711

Murals on the outside of downtown buildings help Algoma explain its history. Pick up a walking tour brochure at the lakeside Visitors Center to find all ten and historically significant structures.

Vacationers in a hurry to get to the better-known Door County peninsula tend to forget Algoma. Such a shame. visitalgomawi.com, (920) 487-2041

Charter fishing is an option in Algoma and 10 miles south in Kewaunee, population 2,837, a rugged waterfront town with understated charms. **Tugboat Ludington**, a World War II vessel in Normandy for the D-Day invasion, is open May to October for self-guided tours. kewaunee.org, (920) 388-4822

recipe for cherry wine, earned double gold and best-of-class awards in one of the nation's largest professional wine competitions.

Newer is a line of hard ciders, made with apples from a nearby orchard since 2016. Next came hard ciders with cherries and guava; apples fermented with tequila, bourbon. Open since June 2022 is a cider house, next to the winery, "to give guests another location to enjoy our wines and ciders," says co-owner Brad Schmiling.

Expect free music outdoors at von Stiehl on most summer Fridays and Saturdays. The annual Wet Whistle Wine Fest, in mid-September, adds a grape stomp—and some winery fans show up in zany costumes that include dressing as a wine bottle.

It's a high-spirited gathering to complement reports of spirits that linger within winery walls. Ask about "Henry," an immigrant from Germany and Civil War veteran who used the building as a brewery so long ago.

Baileys Harbor

Population 1,223

The Ridges Sanctuary

ridgessanctuary.org
(920) 839-2802

The dwarf lake iris has sat on the federal list of threatened plants since 1988, but I know where it grows like a weed in May and vanishes before summer arrives.

Hundreds of the tiny blue-purple flowers, most no bigger than a thumbnail, mingle among junipers and pop through sand at The Ridges Sanctuary, Baileys Harbor. Each delicate petal is a marvel with three splashes of deep yellow per bloom.

The species is but one example of what makes these 1,600-plus acres extraordinary. The sanctuary is a National Natural Landmark, one of eighteen in Wisconsin, and the area is known for having the most plants in the state that are rare.

The Ridges also is Wisconsin's oldest nonprofit nature preserve, a place of research as well as protection. Between each of thirty ridges are swales—marshy depressions—that create a patchwork of habitats unusual for a condensed area.

Each ridge represents a former Lake Michigan shoreline, the oldest dating back 1,200 years. As shoreline recedes, vegetation sprouts and eventually morphs into boreal forests. The ridges continue to form at the water's edge, in thirty- to fifty-year cycles; species tend to thrive here instead of fade away.

Efforts to protect the acreage began in 1937 with 30-acre Baileys Harbor Ridges Park, whose two range lights would assist in the navigation of Lake Michigan ships.

Milwaukee botanist Albert Fuller and landscape architect Jens Jensen teamed up to prevent the area from becoming a trailer

NIAGARA ESCARPMENT

Wisconsin state legislature declared 2010 as the year of the **Niagara Escarpment**, a reference to 230 miles of often-steep ledges and cliffs that skirt through six Wisconsin counties, then underwater in Lake Michigan.

The 1,000-mile escarpment—an ancient sea bottom, created through erosion before glacier movement—stretches through Ontario, Canada, and as far east as New York. The escarpment is named after the cliff over which the Niagara River plunges into Niagara Falls. escarpmentnetwork.org

When in Door County, look for escarpment formations along the two-mile Eagle Trail in **Peninsula State Park**. Although described as a difficult hike, it's easily managed in dry weather and when approached counterclockwise. The Department of Natural Resources occasionally conducts guided hikes and dubs Eagle Trail as the park's most spectacular.

Another park highlight: climbing one hundred steps or following a gently sloped ramp to the top of Eagle Tower, 230 feet above ground. dnr.wi.gov, (920) 868-3258

campground, a change that would have forever compromised natural habitats.

Those orchids? Ridges staff have documented twenty-eight of the state's forty native orchid species at the sanctuary. An orchid restoration project is ongoing and pursued in partnership with the North American Orchid Conservation Center, among others.

"We have sent our folks to England to do this work—which began in 2015—and have partnered with the Smithsonian and others to study orchid restoration," says Katie Krouse, director of operations.

Generic issues include neighborhood integrity and public awareness. Manure run-off from farms, beachfront lawn mowing, and the threat of non-native plants—invasive species such as garlic mustard and buckthorn—are challenges.

So is making more people aware of The Ridges. Those efforts heighten appreciation for nature and boost financial support but also increase habitat vulnerability—no matter how many boardwalks are built as footpaths. (The newest, Hidden Brook Boardwalk, is one-third mile and accessible to all.)

IN THE NEIGHBORHOOD

The more rugged east shore of the Door Peninsula arguably draws a quieter and more contemplative crowd.

Baileys Harbor Range Lights were in service for a century, until 1969, and restored in 1993. Look for them at The Ridges. At the north end of Baileys Harbor is **Cana Island Lighthouse**, established in 1869 and accessible by walking across a stone causeway.

These beacons are among the eleven in Door County; lighthouse festivals happen in spring and fall. dcmm.org, (920) 743-5958

Lovers of nature are a good fit for fifteen-room **Blacksmith Inn on the Shore**, where rooms overlook Lake Michigan, and hammocks swing on private balconies. Follow the boardwalk, over marshland, from shore to pier. Room rates include continental breakfast, starring house-made granola and fresh bakery. theblacksmithinn.com, (920) 839-9222

Chefs at **Chives Door County** make bread to ice cream from scratch. Soup to sausage, too, in a fine-dining setting. On an adjacent property is the restaurant's seasonal food truck court, with full bar service and serving salads in a jar, pizzas from a wood-fired oven. chivesdoorcounty.com, (920) 839-2000

Harbor Fish Market and Grille is known for its three-course lobster dinner, reservations recommended. Expect lobster bisque, a 2-pound boiled lobster with baby reds, cob of corn, mussels, and clams. For dessert: cherry bread pudding. harborfishmarket-grille.com, (920) 839-9999

At **Door County Brewing Company**—a fifteen-barrel brewery—is an indoor music hall, outdoor beer garden, and smart experimentation for what's on tap. One choice: Velvet Bulldozer, an imperial stout. doorcountybrewingco.com, (920) 412-7226

Since 1997, **Stone's Throw Winery** culls California grapes to produce many of the wines served and sipped on an 8-acre estate. Try the Petit Verdot, a double-gold winner in international competition. stonesthrowwinery.com, (920) 839-9660

For more about the area: doorcounty.com, (920) 743-4456.

Five miles of hiking trails are open from dawn to dusk; adults who are not members of The Ridges pay a trail fee. Options for children include a summer camp and nature preschool.

Guided field trips occur all year. The sanctuary hosts the Door County Festival of Nature in late May; programming extends throughout the peninsula. Wreath making, luminaries, caroling, and treats—such as chestnuts roasting over a campfire—are part of Natural Christmas, a newer tradition.

"Baileys Harbor is on the map because of The Ridges," said Andy Gill, executive director, but in Door County "lots of people and institutions are protecting the land. People come here because of that. Natural resources are all around you."

At least 32,000 acres, 5 percent of the total in Door County, are protected by government and nonprofit entities. Unknown additional acres are protected by private landowners who are passionate about conservation.

Boulder Junction

Population 179

Ghost Deer

boulderjct.org
(715) 385-2400

As sunset nears, I slow for a couple of we-own-the-place deer that bolt in front of my car in downtown Boulder Junction. Then comes a third. Anybody else around?

Such occurrences are not uncommon in this stylish but secluded hamlet, surrounded by **Northern Highland American Legion State Forest**, **Chequamegon-Nicolet National Forest** and, in Michigan, **Ottawa National Forest**.

Much more unpredictable is a fleeting glimpse of the marquee cousin to the ordinary brown whitetails. In the area live albino deer, identifiable by their white coat, pink or light blue eyes, pink nose and hooves. Also known as "ghost deer," as of 2022 they are a protected animal and illegal to hunt. Color of hooves, eyes, and nose distinguish them from other white deer.

Boulder Junction Chamber of Commerce promotes the rare albino as a reason to visit, but you have to know where to look and aren't guaranteed a sighting. Ask the chamber where the deer have shown up lately and be respectful of private property boundaries.

Like most wildlife, the deer tend to move at dawn and dusk. Consider them a photographer's dream, beautiful and mystical creatures that—although white—can stand out during winter's backdrop of snow.

Native Americans attach spiritual significance to white deer. Nature photographer Jeff Richter of Mercer (population 551), 24 miles west, documents the species in his 2007 book *White Deer: Ghosts of the Forest*, with text by area naturalist John Bates. naturespressbooks.com

Much remains a mystery. In 2000, the state Department of Natural Resources asked, via Facebook: "Have you seen an albino or white deer around Wisconsin recently? We're looking to get a better understanding of where they live around the state." In the nearly 300 replies were many photos of white deer spotted in various parts of Wisconsin.

Jeffrey Pritzl, DNR deer program specialist, says there is no way to accurately determine the white deer population. Sightings were reported in twenty-four counties, "so this demonstrates that white deer may not be as rare as some believe," but he believes the total is well below 1 percent of all deer in Wisconsin.

"There are a couple of areas in the state where white deer can be seen regularly," Jeffrey says, "but the Northwoods setting and Boulder Junction (as an attractive travel destination) make the occurrences there stand out."

The white deer population likely is growing "since white deer are currently protected statewide and able to pass on genetics that create more white deer."

FAST FIVE

Boutiques and bistros are an unexpected contrast to Boulder Junction's remote location. Most are within two blocks and stay open all year.

Moondeer and Friends Gallery sells fine art and folk art from dozens of regional artists. Fiber specialists hook rugs, paint on silk, weave, create jewelry and soft sculptures. Carvers make burl bowls, decoys, and clocks from wood. Find antler sculptures and painted gourds in addition to photography, paintings, other customary art forms. moondeergallery.com, (715) 385-2082

On tap at **Aqualand Alehouse** are up to twenty kinds of craft beer: quaff them with wood-fired pizza. "Aqualand" refers to a beloved but now-closed animal park. Look for live music in the beer garden during summer. aqualandalehouse.com, (715) 385-0380

The Guide's Inn serves pan-fried walleye, house-made ice cream, and riffs on Wellingtons (beef, chicken, salmon, vegetarian) that reflect founder Jimmy Dean Van Rossum's Culinary Institute of America training. Fine, leisurely dining in a backwoods setting. "Guide" refers to fishing guides. theguidesinn.com, (715) 385-2233

Peeplelures is not simply a jewelry store. Showstoppers are wearable art, handcrafted and individually designed by individuals, and upscale brands. Made with an array of gemstones and materials beyond silver and gold. Think brass, bronze, copper, niobium, pewter. peeplelures.com, (715) 385-0100

Coontail Adventures sells and rents most of whatever is necessary for enjoying the Northwoods. That includes skis, snowshoes, fat-tire bikes, canoes, kayaks, paddleboards, and attire/gear to look good, function. coontail.com, (888) 874-0885

At protectthewhitedeer.com, hunters and nonhunters 325 miles south of Boulder Junction advocate for continued preservation of the animal. The website cites research findings that 1 in 20,000 to 1 in 30,000 whitetail deer is born albino.

In Boulder Junction, the unusual deer gives humans good reason to stay alert while hiking, biking, fishing, or kayaking. Many of the 194 lakes within a 10-mile radius of the community are surrounded by forest.

That means peaceful surroundings where many species take refuge. **Heart of Vilas County**, a paved and 52-mile bike trail, is one way to get acquainted with inhabitants. Boulder Junction is near the route's halfway point. biketheheart.org

THE MUSKY FIGHT

Boulder Junction and Hayward, population 2,533, both make the muskellunge (Wisconsin's official state fish) a part of their identity. An 8-foot-long chainsaw carving of the fish, called "Gill," is outside the Chamber of Commerce. Another bigger-than-life musky is painted onto a propane tank.

A 1971 court decree declared Boulder Junction the Musky Capital of the World, a title that nemesis Hayward also sought; the battle took more than twenty years to complete. More than fifty lakes in the area are rated Class A for musky.

Fishing guides in Boulder Junction introduce visitors to area lakes for free during the 3-day **Musky Jamboree** in August. The annual event is the community's biggest, and the same guides conduct free weekly fishing seminars in June through August.

In business since 1926 is friendly **Headwaters**, a tavern and restaurant on a hill overlooking the Manitowish River where it links Boulder and Little Rice lakes. Take a fishing break or paddle over on a canoe. Expect authentic Northwoods décor: above the fireplace is a framed charcoal drawing of fishing guides at a shore lunch. Serving sandwiches to steak/seafood dinners. On Facebook, (715) 385-2601

Eagle River

Population 1,628

World Championship Snowmobile Derby

derbycomplex.com
(715) 479-4424

The chill of winter is what brings on the fever in Vilas County, where 600-some miles of groomed snowmobile trails link communities, sashay through forests, cut across lakes, and quickly find wilderness.

The joy of riding—to appreciate nature and solitude or hop from rural bar to supper club with friends—is enough for most snowmobilers. The thrill of speed and precision challenges others: they come to Eagle River, the county seat, where championship racing on snow and ice began in 1964.

That snowmobile race was a resort operator's way to drum up winter business for Chanticleer Inn. He hoped for a few dozen spectators and got 2,000, who watched one hundred snowmobiles zoom on Dollar Lake.

A quarter-mile oval track was built the next winter. Before the decade ended, the track expanded to one-half mile, and farm tractors

were topping it with snow and sawdust. "Artificial snow wasn't an option back then," recalls Howard "Rusty" Wolf, who raced. "It was very rough—if you fell, you felt it."

By the early 1970s, Eagle River was known as Snowmobiling Capital of the World, and now the annual derby encompasses three days, several racing events (one for vintage models) and speeds pushing 100 mph. Snowmobiles zip atop 18 to 20 inches of ice that is shaved and smoothed over the high-banked, oval track.

FAST FIVE

Snowmobile Hall of Fame and Museum, St. Germain, population 2,083, is the keeper of historically significant snowmobiles and stories of people who helped put snowmobiling on the map. snowmobilehalloffame.com, (715) 542-4463

Inside World Snowmobile Headquarters in Eagle River are the **International Snowmobile Hall of Fame** that recognizes snowmobile evolution and achievements in the sport and industry and the **Antique Snowmobile Club of America Museum**, for vintage to high-tech models. worldsnowmobilinghq.com, (715) 479-2186

Another stop for lovers of icy sports: **Wisconsin Hockey Hall of Fame**, inside Eagle River Sports Arena, collects memorabilia and honors leaders in the growth of amateur ice hockey. That includes exceptional players, coaches, sports officials. wihockeyhalloffame.com

When winter weather cooperates, look for a **20-foot-tall ice castle** downtown, an annual labor of love for the Eagle River Volunteer Fire Department. Colored lights brighten the edifice at night.

For more about the area: vilaswi.com, (715) 479-3649; eagleriver.org, (715) 479-6400.

Before the derby begins, a brass torch is carried to Eagle River by snowmobilers who stop at more than a dozen snowmobile clubs en route. When there's not enough snow, Rusty says "we drive our pickup trucks." Either way, the ritual takes two days.

"It's like car racing—expensive," Rusty says, of those who race their sleek, motorized sleds at the Eagle River derby. The world's first snowmobile, built nearby in 1924, wasn't much more than a glorified toboggan. Carl Eliason, his mobility limited by a chronic foot problem, invented the device and patented it three years later. eliason-snowmobile.com

Model T parts, bicycle parts, a boat motor, and skis were cobbled together so the inventor could more easily check his traplines. Word got around fast, and the patent was sold when an order for 200 of the contraptions came from Finland. Look for the original snowmobile at Vilas Historical Museum in Sayner, population 231, 20 miles northwest of Eagle River and open May through September. vilasmuseum.com

Rusty cofounded one of the first snowmobile clubs in Wisconsin, whose membership began with six couples and grew to 525 families, some as far away as California. Now known as Sno-Eagles, it is one of eleven snowmobile clubs in Vilas County and 600-some in the state.

The task of keeping trails groomed isn't a casual commitment. "They don't just follow roads or ditches—many are 16 feet wide" and cut into national/state forests, sometimes as forestry roads and fire lanes that are not plowed during winter. Volunteers from the nonprofit clubs monitor conditions and do the work; equipment and fuel are subsidized by local fund-raisers and state money from snowmobile registrations.

IN THE NEIGHBORHOOD

The hot spot for entertainment and visual arts in **Three Lakes**, population 605, is **Three Lakes Center for the Arts**, whose art deco theater is in a Quonset hut designed and built by baseball great Cy Williams (he is buried in Three Lakes Cemetery). The structure is one of six nationwide that still show movies. tlcfa.org, threelakes.com, (715) 546-3344

In **Woodruff**, population 891, is the **Dr. Kate Museum**, which tells the story of the "Angel on Snowshoes" who walked to reach patients when winter roads were undrivable. In her 1950s quest to build a hospital, the area's children collected a million pennies, and a *This Is Your Life* segment brought enough additional donations to complete the project. Open June to September. drkatemuseum.org, (715) 356-6896

PLENTY FOR SUPPER

Supper club dining—leisurely and hearty steak/seafood meals at a family-run operation—is a Wisconsin tradition, especially in the North-woods. Expect to make a night of it: most supper clubs don't take reservations, and customers expect to wait an hour or longer for a table. Settle in with an Old Fashioned cocktail, chill, and get acquainted with talking to strangers. End the night with a grasshopper or other ice-cream drink. It's all part of the supper club experience, and there are dozens of Northwoods choices.

For starters, consider this range of rural locations:

El Capitan, Florence, population 641—Owned by the same family since 1959 and known for Italian entrées in addition to traditional supper club fare. That means house-made pasta, meatballs, sauce, and bread. elcapitansupperclub.com, (715) 696-3493

Little Bohemia Lodge, Manitowish Waters, population 624—John Dillinger and Baby Face Nelson escaped from an FBI shootout here in 1934. Bullet holes remain in the building, a filming site for the 2009 *Public Enemies*. Look for artifacts from the era. littlebohemialodge .com, (715) 543-8800

Marty's Place North, Woodruff, population 891—Count roast duck with a cherry currant demi-glace among the signature entrées. For the big eater: New York strips, pork chops, and rib eyes that each weigh in at 12 ounces. martysplacenorth.com, (715) 356-4335

Norwood Pines, Minocqua—A good place to land in all seasons: take a seat beside the fireplace or on the screened porch. Friday fish fry comes with corn fritters. Seafood-stuffed salmon, racks of ribs, and cheesecakes are other specialties. norwoodpines.com, (715) 356-3666

Pitlik's, Eagle River—In the same family since 1928, when the resort on Sand Lake was bought from Charles Comis-key of the Chicago White Sox. Now a fifth generation of Pitliks is involved. Fish on Fridays is called a "shore lunch" of walleye, bluegill, haddock, or shrimp. pitliksresort.com, (833) 748-5457

Ullman's Ding-A-Ling, Mercer (population 551)—Count the Food Network among this supper club's fans. Flower boxes hang outside; diners cozy up at the horseshoe bar inside. Order walleye broiled or beer-battered and fried on Fridays. Share a Brandy Alexander for dessert. On Facebook, (715) 476-2270

White Stag Inn, Sugar Camp (population 1,819)—Open since 1956 and proud of unchanging traditions: meats cook on charcoal broilers. Served with a baked potato. Salad is a wedge of iceberg lettuce, topped with secret dressings (sold by the jar, too). Outside is a big, white elk statue. (715) 272-1057

Twice a week during winter, Rusty says a Sno-Eagle member will lead visiting snowmobilers on a ride of 100 to 150 miles. They meet in the morning, stop for lunch, and make a day of it. snoeagles.org

Rent a snowmobile in Eagle River if you don't have one, but how hard is the vehicle to operate? Sometimes it's all about the journey, not the distance. Rusty says a guy called from Chicago because he and friends wanted to try snowmobiling but needed a guide in addition to equipment.

"All four were from India," Rusty recalls. "We drove to lunch, a distance that would take me 30 or 40 minutes, but that became the full outing. They kept stopping to take pictures of wildlife, or would miss a turn, but had the times of their lives."

Egg Harbor

Population 358

Chief Oshkosh Native American Arts

facebook.com/chiefoshkosh
(920) 621-7343

One of our last stops during a girlfriend getaway to Door County was almost an afterthought. "That place with the teepee has been there forever," a friend remarked. The rest of us knew what she was talking about but didn't recall ever stepping inside.

Trendy products, catchy business names, and stylish storefronts are a part of what makes Wisconsin's much-loved peninsula a boutique shopper's dream, but Egg Harbor's **Chief Oshkosh Native American Arts** is different. Outside are a couple of weathered totem poles, and the shop is a simple log building, painted dark brown with white trim.

Nothing flashy, but inside are treasures: traditional handicrafts and fine art, made by Native Americans in Wisconsin and beyond.

Roy Oshkosh, leader of the state's Menominee Nation, opened the business as the Chief Oshkosh Trading Post around 1950. In the backyard was a 600-seat amphitheater that presented weekly summer powwows at which his Owassie dancers introduced authentic Native American ceremonials. Kids would learn to dance with them near the end of each performance.

The business location was deliberate. "Look in the middle of the peninsula, for a babbling brook running through a wooded glen, then disappearing into the ground and never to be seen again," the grand-mother of Chief Oshkosh had advised. She was describing land that had been a popular summer camp for Native Americans long ago, and her grandson bought the property shortly after he knew he had found it.

The bowl-shaped amphitheater also was the site of Boy Scout camporees until Chief Oshkosh's death in 1974. The business lost its

FAST FIVE

A visit to Door County never seems stale. New businesses always seem to emerge or change their look, emphasis. But there's also a solid foundation of stops that have endured the tests of time and ongoing competition. For example:

Goats play, graze, and butt heads on the sod roof of **Al Johnson's**, home to all that is Scandinavian, especially Swedish. Shop the specialty *butik* while waiting to dine on Swedish pancakes (with lingonberries), Swedish meatballs, pickled herring. In business since 1949 in Sister Bay, population 1,148. aljohnsons.com, (920) 854-2626

If it can be grown in Door County and baked or canned, you'll likely find it at **Bea's Ho-Made Products**, which began business by selling cherries at a road-side stand in 1961. Chopped cherry jam is a signature product. At Gills Rock, population not tracked. beashomade products.com, (920) 854-2268

Sister Bay Bowl, Sister Bay, began business as Sister Bay Hotel, owned by the same family since 1950. Down came a dance hall, up went a six-lane bowling alley and then a supper club menu. A retro look remains, and games are scored manually. sisterbaybowl.com, (920) 854-2841

No inn on the peninsula is older than **The Whistling Swan**, built in 1887 and moved miles across ice to its present location 20 years later. For rent are seven rooms and suites. Match a dinner of chicken schnitzel or lamb ragout with wines from around the world. In Fish Creek, population not tracked. whistlingswan.com, (920) 868-3442

The outdoor fish boil is a summer Door County tradition, and historic **White Gull Inn** in Fish Creek offers the flashy food theater all year, but on multiple days from May through October. Whitefish boils in a cauldron with red potatoes, as settlers did more than a century ago. Add coleslaw, fresh breads, and cherry pie for dessert. whitegullinn.com, (920) 868-3517

distinctiveness as ownership changed, but then an Oneida artist and teacher slowly began refreshing things.

Owner Coleen Bins has elevated the quality of merchandise sold indoors and aims to restore the outdoor theater to its peak of glory. Only mowing and stone steps provided hints about the grassy amphitheater's past before fund-raising began.

The first fund-raiser concert was by Joanne Shenandoah, a Grammy Award winner and New York Oneida who helped deepen Coleen's understanding of Oneida heritage and history. The two women got to know each other while Coleen worked on a master's degree from Rochester Institute of Technology in New York.

"My education not only took place in the university," she says. "I got an education in our traditions as well," and the Shenandoah family was instrumental in this process.

Instead of cheap souvenirs that reinforce Native American stereotypes—tomahawks, bows and arrows, phony peace pipes—Coleen sells traditional crafts and fine art made by Native Americans.

"I concentrate on the Woodland region of native peoples since our art is all about our surrounding environment," she says. In her inventory are works by watercolorist Dawn Dark Mountain of Madison, painter Mary Prescott, dollmaker Judith Jourdan of Oneida, and many others. Some of these artists excel in more than one medium.

Wooden flutes, birch bark baskets and canoes, hand-beaded and silver jewelry, indigenous music CDs, and herbal blends are among the other items sold.

"We have decided to do (amphitheater restoration) the way Roy did it, with the help of others. That way it belongs to many," Coleen explains. Her intention was to approach the Menominee Nation early on: "We want to ask people who understand what we have to offer to help us first."

Why are the amphitheater and retail business important to her? She expressed frustration with the disrespect and lack of knowledge associated with Native American history, culture, and traditions.

"I want Native people to share their stories with the public the way Roy did," Coleen says. "Now, and finally, instead of someone interpreting who we are and what we do . . . we can talk about ourselves and share in a respectful way."

In addition to operating the Chief Oshkosh shop, Coleen returned to the Oneida in Wisconsin in 1994 to teach arts and heritage for twelve years. The metalsmith artist, who also works in other mediums, remains a guest teacher whose travels acquaint children and adults about Native American art.

Ellison Bay

Population 249

The Clearing Folk School

theclearing.org
(920) 854-4088

Some folks seek a new destination for each trip they take. Others go to the same place year after year, or multiple times per year, to deepen a connection to a setting, community, or their own creative energy.

Most come to The Clearing's 128 acres, near the tip of Door County, to learn something new or practice what they don't make time for at home. It could be quilting or forging, creative writing or bird watching, philosophy or photography—with whatever subject comes an opportunity to lighten the heart, touch the soul.

They follow a curvy road to a slower pace of life and typically share family-style meals. One price covers lodging, most meals, and a class.

"We think it's a bargain," says Michael Schneider, executive director. "And it's a comfortable, safe place to be." On the property are hiking trails, prime views of Lake Michigan sunsets, historic buildings, lodging, woods, and meadowland.

"We're still not too big, and that's a comfort," he says. When we meet in late September, much of the following summer's schedule already is reserved for specific classes and instructors. In winter, day classes are geared more toward local residents, who return home at night.

"This was to landscape architect students what Frank Lloyd Wright and Taliesin were to architecture students," Michael explains. Migrations to The Clearing began in 1935 under the tutelage of Jens Jensen, whose work in nature preservation and conservation earned international respect.

Instruction, then and now, is noncompetitive and interdisciplinary. Regardless of class topic, history, creativity, interaction with nature, and quiet contemplation are likely involved.

MORE ART APPRECIATION

Peninsula Players is the oldest resident summer theater in the nation. Performances began on a two-plank stage in 1935 and grew into an open-air venue with movable walls in a cedar forest with waterfront setting. June into October. peninsulaplayers.com, (920) 868-3287

The original and endearingly quirky musicals of **Northern Sky Theater** began in 1990 and tend to pay attention to Wisconsin culture (examples: *Dad's Season Tickets*, about Green Bay Packer loyalties; *Guys on Ice*, about ice fishing). Addition of an indoor theater in 2019 extended the production season. northernskytheater.com, (920) 854-6117

Both theaters are near Fish Creek, not a census designated location.

Classical theater is the specialty of **Door Shakespeare**, which performs during a part of summer in the garden of Björklunden, a large estate facing Lake Michigan at Baileys Harbor, population 334. The property is a part of Lawrence University. doorshakespeare.com, (920) 854-7111

In Door County are more than one hundred art galleries and studios. Make your own mark at **Hands On Art Studio**, converted farm buildings that are a roomy and family-friendly place to make mosaics, glassware, sculptures, paintings, jewelry. Near Fish Creek. handsonartstudio.com, (920) 868-9311

For more about the area: doorcounty.com, (920) 743-4456.

When the Danish American founder died in 1951, Wisconsin Farm Bureau managed the acreage, and types of classes changed. Chicago academics helped mold the property's mission to emphasize the humanities: literature, philosophy, the arts.

"The audience has evolved," Michael says, from students in their 20s to an average age of 65 to 70. Many are repeat visitors, and class capacity is relatively small.

A new workshop, built in 2007, means four classes can happen simultaneously. A former garage became a workshop for carving and stained-glass classes. Elsewhere is a large schoolhouse and weaving studio. The dining room seats forty.

The mood is peaceful, laid-back, and harmonious. "People check their politics and religion at the door," Michael says. "We don't need to tell them—they do this on their own."

Docent-led tours of the campus happen on many weekends, May through October, and last 2 hours. Only the visitor center bookstore and gift shop are open at other times, so the property stays private for retreat students.

Ephraim

Population 345

Preserving the Past

ephraim.org
(920) 854-4989

Much distinguishes Ephraim from other locales in tourist-friendly Door County.

The local yacht club—organized in 1906—is one of the oldest on the Great Lakes, but the actual structure is tiny. Anyone can join, including nonresidents, and children begin sailing lessons at age 7. Ephraim's annual **Flying Scots Regatta**, in August, is among the largest of its type in the nation.

The village has the county's longest stretch of public lakeshore access and, until 2016, Ephraim was the only dry community remaining in Wisconsin. Referenda overturned a 163-year ban on alcohol sales after similar attempts failed in 1934 and 1992.

As village president Mike McCutcheon told me at the time, "We're not going to be the biker capital of Wisconsin, but this will help our restaurants." He acknowledged that some local residents didn't want Ephraim to change. "We want to be sensitive and smart about it, and we don't want to change the character of Ephraim."

Which brings us to another trait that separates Ephraim from the rest: a robust interest in local history and preservation. Eleven of thirty local historical sites are on the National Register of Historic Places. Some galleries and shops operate out of well-kept old buildings.

Passionate volunteers lead guided, 90-minute history tours that include **Anderson Store** (built in 1858), **Ephraim Moravian Church** (1858), **Anderson Barn** (1880), and **Pioneer Schoolhouse** (1880). These **Ephraim Historical Foundation** tours happen on foot or on tram, from late spring into autumn. Reservations advised.

The area was settled by Norwegian Moravians, a faith community whose founder "wanted to preach and read scripture in the language of the people he served," explains local historian Linda Carey, whose ancestors arrived here in 1880.

Ephraim still has a hundred-member Moravian congregation that "resembles a Methodist or Presbyterian church today," and the community's longtime no-alcohol rule "was more a part of the times than a part of the Moravian" teachings.

MORE DEEP HISTORY

Wilson's in Ephraim, an old-time soda fountain with juke boxes and flame-kissed burgers, began business in 1906. Look for the red and white striped awnings. Open mid-May to mid-October. wilsonsicecream.com, (920) 854-2041

Near the village is **Skyway Drive-in Theatre**, in business since 1950 and one of the rare remaining outdoor theaters for movies. Open May to early October. doorcountydrivein.com, (920) 854-9938

Moravian church members give away a taste of sugar cake (like a coffee cake, but with holes poked for a butter-brown sugar mix to seep in) during the annual **Fyr** (pronounced "feer") **Ball Festival** on Father's Day weekend in June. Evening bonfires burn the "winter witch" and welcome summer.

Open-air worship with a rotation of clergy, nicknamed the weekly "docks-ology," is a Wednesday night tradition at **Anderson Dock** and Eagle Harbor in July and August; bring your own seating. Add free summer concerts on Monday nights at Harborside Park's gazebo and community singalongs on summer Sunday nights at **Ephraim Village Hall**.

Hurley

Population 1,558

Silver Street

hurleywi.com
(715) 208-0902

Search "Hurley" on the Wisconsin Tavern League website and about twenty-five results pop up. More than half are on Silver Street, a main drag that leads to Michigan and the slightly larger city of Ironwood.

The Badger State loves its beer and bars, but this per capita ratio is over the top—even for us—and it's been that way in Hurley for a century.

The city with a hell-on-wheels reputation pretty much ignored Prohibition. Locals say the area was home to about 130 places to buy alcohol during that era.

Many were along Silver Street, disguised as candy stores and soda fountains. Some stills operated in underground tunnels. Customers included Al Capone and other gangsters, but the bigger base were iron ore miners and lumberjacks who were eager to spend money and unwind when payday arrived.

In Hurley's Iron County are 200 miles of ATV (all-terrain vehicle) trails, and about 80 percent of land is forest. Skiers visit Hurley because of Michigan's Powderhorn Mountain, 8 miles northeast, and other downhill ranges. Deer hunters and snowmobilers know Hurley, too.

All this helps keep the taverns in business. Most don't bother with websites or might not have updated Facebook sites for years. The vibe is friendly, working class, unpretentious.

FAST FACT

In Iron County are eleven waterfalls and half of the ten tallest in Wisconsin. Best known is 90-foot-high Potato River Falls, 20 miles west of Hurley.

FAST FIVE

Gabe Lagalo infuses gourmet twists, international riffs, and from-scratch recipes in meals that comfort at **Kimball Inn**, 5 miles northwest of Hurley. Northwoodsy décor meets high-end quality at an affordable price. Sauced-up and dry-rubbed ribs come from the in-house smoker. On a chalkboard are menu specials: maybe crab-stuffed sole, pork hocks with cabbage, osso buco (with asiago polenta and a tomato demi-glace) all on the same day. Open for dinner. On Facebook, (715) 561-4095

Headquarters for **Iron County Historical Society** is a three-story museum in a Romanesque building that was the county's former courthouse. Save time for the clock tower and weaving room. ironcountymuseum.org, (906) 265-2617

Thick logs from ore docks built the **National Finnish American Festival Cultural Center**, also known as "Little Finland" and just outside of Hurley. The free museum and gift shop are open seasonally. For sale are traditional Finnish sauna buckets and scrubbing brushes, linens, handicrafts, and kitsch. The center is a meeting place for occasional Finnish films, music, dancing and meals (featuring *hernekeitto*—pea soup, *mojakka*—stew, *pannukakku*—oven-baked pancakes). littlefinland.org, (715) 561-4360

At **Plummer Mine Interpretive Park** is a 1904 headframe (to hoist people, materials from an underground mine shaft). It is 80 feet high and the last to still stand in Wisconsin.

Explore the architectural remnants of Montreal, population 801, built as a **utopian mining community** in the 1920s. The town, the only one in Wisconsin specifically designed to house and accommodate iron ore miners and their families, is on the National Register of Historic Places. Although the mine closed in 1962, some mine buildings still stand.

For more about the area: ironcountywi.com, (715) 561-2922.

Gentlemen's bars—strip clubs—are confined by city ordinance to Silver Street's Lower Block, next to the Montreal River. At least two, Idle Hour Saloon and Tails 'n' Trails, have been chamber of commerce members; so has Club Carnival, a shop with X-rated novelties for adults.

Dawn's Never Inn, in the former Santini Hotel, is at the top of the Lower Block, which made for interesting conversation when I met owner Dawn Gresham. "A lot of guys get to the front door, open it, and realize we're not what they're looking for," she told me. "Others come inside to wait for their buddies."

ANOTHER BORDER TOWN

The Paint River separates Florence, population 641, from Upper Michigan in Florence County, where a majority of land is publicly owned and 265 lakes, 165 miles of rivers mean lots of elbow room for fishing, paddling, and swimming.

Stay at **Lakeside Bed and Breakfast**, a roomy and three-story house on Fisher Lake in downtown Florence. Rates include use of kayaks, canoes, paddleboards. The clear lake is neither overdeveloped nor neglected. florencelakesidebb.com, (715) 528-3259

Walk Central Avenue for a little binging on from-scratch bakery, chocolates, jewelry, and gifts at cute shops. Ask where to buy a hand-crafted canoe or stumpf fiddle (a percussion-string instrument, for folk music). There's more depth to discover here than water levels.

On the locals' list of 101 things to do, when I visited: listen to a chorus of frogs, look for animal tracks, wade in a stream, dissect owl pellets, take a child fishing. Find the backstory on the mining and logging town at **Wild Rivers Interpretive Center**. exploreflorencecounty.com, (888) 889-0049

The old hotel's swinging mahogany doors, hand-carved back bar, and leaded glass remain. Some call it the most beautiful bar in the city; others visit because of ghost lore. All separate Dawn's from the competition.

Many of the other Silver Street taverns use signage or other means to distinguish themselves. **Ladder 75** has a firefighter theme. **Mac's Bar** opens at 6 a.m. The setting for **Bank Club** is a historic bank. **Iron Nugget** intends to make its own beer.

Pool and dart tournaments, big-screen TVs for watching sports, live music or karaoke, cheap drink specials, craft brews, and pub grub matter here, too. Although daytime personality might be very different than at nighttime, and business names may change with the years, the spirit of freewheeling Hurley stays pretty much the same from one generation to the next.

Iola

Population 1,249

Iola Car Show

**iolaoldcarshow.com
(715) 445-4000**

What began in 1972 as a way to sell magazine subscriptions quickly accelerated into one of the nation's largest shows for vintage and other vehicles. About 100,000 attend the three-day July event on 300 acres, and $8.5 million in proceeds have benefited many local charities.

"It's been a national-caliber event for decades," says Joe Opperman, executive director, and prospective American car buyers come from as far as China to shop. "I liken it to a family-friendly version of Sturgis," the annual South Dakota pilgrimage for motorcyclists. Both gatherings have repeat visitors because of a strong sense of community and connection.

The nonprofit Iola endeavor involves fewer than ten staffers, thousands of volunteers, and thousands of vendors. "There is no wealthy backer" to make it all happen, Joe says. Similar events usually occur on leased property, but the acreage for this one is a permanent show fixture.

Celebrities, such as Henry "The Fonz" Winkler, and industry icons show up in Iola. So do proud gearheads "who may spend more time restoring, polishing, and tuning up their vehicles than driving them." Cars are their passion, a key part of identity and sometimes their livelihood.

"We are a diverse group of people from every walk of life," Joe says. "We want to appeal to everybody," and that means making room for cars from the late 1800s to new Corvettes.

Visitors cover four generations, and some families turn Iola into their reunion, staying at the grounds' campsites. One longtime attendee donated money to add water and electricity hookups for RVs. Another, a master electrician, donated the labor.

The pandemic canceled the 2020 car show, but 200 vehicles showed up for a fall car rally through the rural area, "just to have something to do to bring people together." Even my little Toyota or a rusted minivan would have been welcome. One year later, 400 vehicles cruised the same route.

We chat in the former headquarters for Krause Publications, a publishing company that Joe says peaked as a $100 million business with 500 employees in Iola. Titles were big on hobby magazines and books, covering many special interests: firearms as well as baseball cards, coins and stamps as well as classic cars. The enterprise was sold to a New York City media company in 2002, and now the Iola buildings are the car show's base.

Founder Chet Krause started with *Numismatic News*, as a newsletter, and expanded from there. In 1971, he launched *Old Cars Weekly* and set out to sell subscriptions by organizing a car show. To boost turnout, he promised to buy attendees a pork chop dinner from the local Lions Club.

Only twenty cars showed up, but within three years the car show outgrew its space. "The bigger it got, the more it became its own business," Joe explains. One that was a marketing deduction for the publisher.

Show cars are assigned a display category: prewar—produced up to 1942 with few or no modifications; postwar—preassembled vehicles from 1945 to 1990; modified—hot rods/kit cars/others from 1990 or earlier; old cars/young drivers—hobbyists under age 25 whose classic vehicles are at least 25 years old; survivor cars—shown as they came from the factory in 1976 or earlier; second-generation specialty cars—those

WORTHY DETOUR

Within 15 miles of Iola is the Waupaca Chain O' Lakes, twenty-two spring-fed bodies of blue-green water that are connected and deep when compared to their surface area. Where to land depends on what makes the perfect day for you.

Otter Lake, one of the smaller ones, is perfect for kayaking but—like a majority of the lakes—not big enough for waterskiing. **Chain Skiers**, a water-ski team, occasionally performs on Rainbow Lake, in front of the Wisconsin Veterans Home. waupacachainskiers.com

Boaters dock at **Clearwater Harbor**, facing Taylor Lake, where music is made on a floating stage during summer. Tour the larger lakes, spring to autumn, on the **Chief Waupaca** paddle wheeler or **Lady of the Lakes** motorized yacht. clearwaterharbor.com, (715) 258-2866

On land, explore Rural, a well-preserved historic district along the Crystal River; Greek Revival and other home styles are on the National Register of Historic Places. The area is largely the same as when settled by Yankees of British descent in the 1850s. Stay at **Crystal River Inn**, a bed-and-breakfast, on an 1853 farmstead. crystalriver-inn.com, (715) 258-5333

For more: explorewaupaca.com, (715) 258-7343.

from 1990 or earlier; and late-model vehicles—unique/prestigious models from 1990 or later.

Vehicles in the Blue Ribbon Concours are there by invitation. Elsewhere is a swap meet and flea market with 4,000 spaces.

Next step: Seek new events that would be a good fit for the area. A concert stage was constructed with this in mind.

Event profits are shared. Iola Lions Club receives $50,000 per year, to use for scholarships and other good deeds. Middle school and high school students years ago got one-to-one access to computer equipment, "an initiative way ahead of its time."

Joe was about 5 years old when his car show work began: his T-ball team helped pick up garbage. That was more than three decades ago. "I think I'm doing exactly what I was made for," he says, of his job to orchestrate the event now.

"What we do here is so much more important than cars and car parts. It's about good works and goodwill."

Lac du Flambeau

Population: 3,552

George W. Brown Jr. Ojibwe Museum and Cultural Center

**ldfmuseum.com
(715) 588-3333**

Peace Pipe Lane. Wild Rice Avenue. Tomahawk Circle.

Lac du Flambeau street signs hint at pride of heritage, and on an ordinary summer weeknight, all seemed uneventful in the remote Vilas County community. Kids played basketball, and parents pushed strollers at Thunderbird Park. Fishing boats bobbed gently as the sun set and a near-full moon rose.

Parking lots were almost full at **The Flame**—a modest bar-restaurant with fry bread, posole-pork soup, decades-old trophy fish mounts—and the more modern **Lake of the Torches** hotel and casino. The two properties are only one-half mile apart but face different lakes. On Facebook, (715) 588-9262; lakeofthetorches.com, (800) 258-6724

AT THE BOWL AND BEYOND

Indian Bowl festivities on July 4 begin with a parade. Concessions typically include Indian tacos, fry bread, and pulled pork. Also popular in summer is the daylong **Bear River Powwow** at Old Indian Village, a major event with participation from most of Wisconsin's Native American nations.

For more about the area: lacduflambeauchamber.com, (715) 588-3346.

In the township are more than one hundred lakes and fewer than 3,500 people, most of whom dwell in simple ranch homes with million-dollar views. It was French fur traders who first called the area Lac du Flambeau, "lake of the torches," a reference to the longtime custom of spearing walleye at night, guided by torchlight.

The Lac du Flambeau Band of Lake Superior Chippewa, who have lived here since 1745, appear quietly proud of their Ojibwe history. About one-half still reside in what is known as Old Indian Village, near Bear River Pow Wow grounds and three miles outside of town, where the river meets Flambeau Lake.

That's one lake over from where I met with Georgine Brown, a self-described "village rat" as a girl. She returned to the land of her parents and grandparents in 2009.

"I thank the Great Spirit every morning for being able to live here," she says. When she kayaks, "it's just a couple of loons and me, waiting for the moon to come up."

Georgine worked for the U.S. Navy in radio communications, then the U.S. Bureau of Indian Affairs, and as a postmaster in Wisconsin's Bad River tribal area. She knows how it feels to be the "token Indian" in a crowd, committee, or interview and wants us to shake that mentality.

It is smarter, Georgine suggests, to see the interconnectedness that makes the world work. Consider Bear River: many lakes drain into the waterway, which eventually ends up in the Mississippi River, then the Gulf of Mexico. So, it's all one in her eyes, and each part holds sacred value.

The tribe's cultural center is named after her father, and the daughter helped the site grow as board president for the adjacent **Waaswaaganing Indian Bowl**. What she sought is a bridge between past and present: "this is for the kids to carry on what we've carried on from our fathers and grandfathers."

AN ARTFUL RETREAT

Not all who live within the 100,000-acre Lac du Flambeau Reservation are Ojibwe. Three miles northeast of Lac du Flambeau village is **Dillman's Bay Resort**, on a quiet peninsula and a frequent location for multiday workshops led by artists from throughout the nation.

Other guests book a room, cabin, condo, or house to simply relax and enjoy the surroundings. "North of the tension zone" is how a brochure describes the longtime family-owned business, which is dog friendly. Open May to October. dillmans.com, (715) 588-3143

Ceremonial dancing and other centuries-old traditions happen at the rebuilt cultural space, an outdoor amphitheater. For the average tribal member, it's a new retreat downtown. For the average traveler, it's a new reason to visit.

Georgine envisions a throwback to intergenerational storytelling and dancing, in addition to an impromptu place for teens to perform, "like a jam or rap session."

The original Indian Bowl, built in 1951, was in such disrepair that it was demolished in 2014. Annual July 4 ceremonial dancing had been a longtime tradition; U.S. President Dwight and Mamie Eisenhower watched it in 1965.

"Pageantry—that's what we're aiming for," Georgine says, of the Indian Bowl reopening. It begins with a blessing of the grounds and arrival of birchbark canoe maker Wayne Valliere by water; he paddles across Long Interlaken Lake, following a torchlit path.

As dancers perform on July 4, a seventeenth-century Waaswaagoning ("lake of flames" in Ojibwe language) village is re-created near the lakeshore. For more than twenty years, such an authentic reproduction of Native American life was open to visitors at a rural site. Think furnished wigwams, a smokehouse, birchbark canoe, ricing pit, firepits, and tools typical for the era.

The tourist attraction closed after extensive damage by vandals and founder Nick Hockings's death in 2012. Situating a new Waaswaagoning inside of the village means more eyes monitor it.

SOVEREIGN NATIONS

In Wisconsin are eleven federally recognized tribal nations, which Native
American Tourism of Wisconsin says is
the largest concentration of tribes in
one state. Each participates in cultural
events open to the public, and their
territory totals 500,000 acres.

The sovereign nations are the Bad River Ojibwe, Forest County
Potawatomi, Ho Chunk, Lac Courte Oreilles Band of Ojibwe, Lac du
Flambeau Band of Lake Superior Chippewa, Menominee Nation, Mole
Lake Sokaogon Chippewa, Oneida Nation, Red Cliff Band of Ojibwe,
St. Croix Band of Ojibwe, and Stockbridge-Munsee Band of Mohicans.
natow.org

The Menominee, stewards for the
largest single area of virgin timber in
Wisconsin, have earned an international reputation for sustainable forest
management. On the reservation is
the **Menominee Logging Museum**,
open May through October, whose
seven log buildings explain more.
menominee-nsn.gov, (715) 799-5258

The museum is near Keshena, population 1,257, and Menominee
County—at 4,255 residents—is the least populated of seventy-two Wisconsin counties.

The waterfront cornerstone since 1989 is the Ojibwe museum, where
exhibits include a 24-foot dugout canoe, a replica fur trading post, and
dioramas of the four seasons, each a scene of Native American life long
ago. A video explains wild rice, fish, and game harvesting—all ongoing
traditions.

For sale in the gift shop are traditional handicrafts made by local and
other Native Americans. Also in the area are excellent Ojibwe artists,
Georgine says, "but many are bashful" or don't have the means to set up
a studio for travelers to visit. She wants that to change.

The next phase of the Indian Bowl project includes an art gallery,
classrooms for learning beadwork to basketry, and a welcome center. "It
costs a lot to think big on a project like this," Georgine acknowledges.
Project donations are welcome. indianbowlproject.org

Minocqua

Population 411

Min-Aqua Bats

minaquabats.com
(715) 575-9754

Short season, deep history, intense interest. That sums up waterskiing in Wisconsin, deemed Water Skiing Capital of the World by a federation for the sport. Doesn't matter that climate usually confines the activity to summer, or less: a national water-ski association consistently has more Upper Midwest members than anywhere else.

Of the 600-plus water-ski clubs nationwide, Min-Aqua Bats has stayed intact the longest, since 1950. In the group are fourth-generation skiers, ages preteen to mid-20s. Some members live out of state or are international. Minocqua is well represented, but so is Florida.

The club presents an ambitious three water-ski shows per week at the **Aqua Bowl**, downtown bleachers facing Minocqua Lake. A bucket is passed for donations, to help cover expenses. Parents sell concessions and merchandise. Sponsorships are the biggest revenue source, and each skier pays yearly dues ($100 in 2022).

FAST FACT

Minocqua, a census-designated place, is inside the town of Minocqua (population 5,062).

"The draw to Minocqua is the place itself, the small and sincere feeling of the community," says Isabelle Boyer, 2022 club president. "We're all part of the community, and the Min-Aqua Bats are part of Minocqua's fabric."

Her great-uncle was a founder of the Bats, and the club is unusual because its members handle all aspects of the shows. Leadership changes as skiers attend college or begin a career, but pride runs deep, and friendships are long-lasting. About 400 club alums returned to celebrate the group's seventieth summer of water-ski shows, and work has begun for a Min-Aqua Bats movie.

AUTUMN DETOUR

Thirty miles south on US 51 is Tomahawk, population 3,441, whose annual **Tomahawk Fall Ride** averages 40,000 motorcycle riders and fans. When Mother Nature cooperates, the multiday gathering in September happens as autumn colors peak.

In the city is a Harley-Davidson Motor Company factory, open for summer tours before the pandemic. The fall rally began in 1982, one year after a few riders (including Harley exec Willie Davidson) took a cruise along scenic backroads near Tomahawk.

The Thunder Parade follows a 17-mile route through city and country. Spectators line up throughout and cheer on state troopers on motorcycles, then military vets and bike clubs. Some wear funny costumes or carry a mascot. The record: 752 motorcycles in the parade.

Bands play on both ends of Main Street, day and night. Vendors sell food, drink, and merchandise. Bars at the outskirts of town arrange music, swap meets, poker runs (riders collect a card at each stop along a route). tomahawkfallride.com

ANIMAL ATTRACTIONS

Wildlife educators lead guided tours at **Northwoods Wildlife Center**, where injured raptors are rescued and rehabilitated. Those that can't return to the wild—be they painted turtles or bald eagles—stay as resident ambassadors. northwoodswildlifecenter.org, (715) 356-7400

Feed a giraffe, watch an endangered snow leopard, and be greeted by parakeets at **Wildwood Wildlife Park Zoo and Safari**, where animal encounters are more up-close and personal than at the average zoo. Tour by foot, tram ride, or paddleboat. At 259 acres and 229 species, Wildwood is the second-largest zoo in Wisconsin (after Milwaukee's). Open seasonally. wildwoodwildlifepark.com, (715) 356-5588

For more about the area: minocqua.org, (715) 356-5266.

"We have one of the best venues in the Midwest for waterskiing," Isabelle believes. Spectators arrive by boat or foot to watch. Being downtown and having good amplification "means the whole town can hear" show narration.

The first person to water-ski did it in 1922 on Lake Pepin, between Minnesota and Wisconsin. The Minocqua club formed after daredevil friends drew crowds while waterskiing on Sundays. By 1952, the American Water Ski Association was bringing its national tournament to Minocqua Lake.

Wisconsin has about thirty water-ski clubs, and Minocqua's likes to be known as creative tricksters who introduce new formations or maneuvers on water. Things such as a slalom pyramid of girls, or partners who can flip one skier onto the shoulders of the other. Isabelle says both stunts emerged during the club's early years.

When not performing, specialty clinics help advance levels of skill in barefoot skiing, pyramid building, and other niches. A few Bats will go on to ski for collegiate teams, or professionally. At least one—Lynn Novakofski—turned what he learned into a longtime career.

The Min-Aqua Bat from 1959 to 1966 is in the USA Water Ski and Wake Sports Foundation Hall of Fame. He was hired as a skier and promoted to show director during his twenty-two years of daily water-ski shows at Cypress Gardens in Florida.

As inaugural president of the National Show Ski Association, Lynn helped develop show skiing rules still used today. That's a huge step from where he began: learning to water-ski at age eight in Minocqua.

"At one point, we had more skiers (at Cypress Gardens) than anywhere else combined," Lynn recalls. As show director, he routinely would return to Wisconsin to recruit water-skiers because they were proficient and conditioned to perform often.

"Those kids are all about having fun—they're not driven as much by tournaments," he says, of the Min-Aqua Bats. "To me, having fun is what it's all about."

Peshtigo

Population 3,420

Peshtigo Fire Museum

peshtigofiremuseum.com
(715) 582-3244

Only a profoundly significant incident would stay referenced on a newspaper's front page for more than 150 years. Consider the somber

details: 1 million acres burned. At least 1,200 lives lost. A community's dreams destroyed, in minutes.

"The City Reborn from the Ashes of America's Most Disastrous Forest Fire." That is how the *Peshtigo Times* frames the lumber town's heritage and character.

The catastrophic Peshtigo Fire on October 8, 1871, gets overlooked in the wider world because the less-deadly but better-publicized Great Chicago Fire happened the same day, killing 300 and gutting 2,100 acres of the bigger city, leaving 100,000 homeless.

Chicago's population in 1871 was 324,000. Peshtigo's was 1,700.

"In 1870, the wood industry was the heartbeat of this area," explains Pauline King, curator at Peshtigo Fire Museum. Chicago's first mayor, William Ogden, owned the Peshtigo Company, a lumber mill and nation's largest producer of woodenware—shingles, broom handles, buckets, and more.

All that remained after the fire were the contents of a fireproof safe or, as Pauline tells it, "the ledger with the company's debts."

Before the incident, the area's last measurable rain was in early July. Although it was not unusual for the people in Peshtigo to deal with fire during the summer of 1871, because of the drought the October blaze was different.

Tornado-level winds from a cold front, Pauline says, increased the velocity of an evening blaze, and "it wiped out the area in an hour." It was a storm of fire, especially devastating in this heavily wooded area, part of a wild frontier.

The few who survived fled, in nightclothes, to the Peshtigo River and dipped themselves into cold water all through the night to avoid being burned or overcome with smoke.

SUCH A SLICE

Fifteen miles south of Peshtigo is **River City Diner and Smokehouse**, Oconto, where pie rules the dessert menu. Baker Caroline Imig has won more than thirty blue ribbons at the National Pie Championships, and diner choices change frequently. The Pie Queen began baking dozens of pies per week after her husband was killed in a farm equipment accident in 1995; she became a single mom with five children.

River City's barbecued meats earn fans, too, from smoked combo platters for dinner to smoked brisket hash for breakfast.
rivercityoconto.com, (920) 835-4262

"When they finally could leave the river at dawn," Pauline says, "they rolled over and over on the riverbanks, to try and get warm again."

When the volunteer-run museum opened in the 1960s, it was a way for locals to make sure the story of Peshtigo wouldn't die. Most amazing are display cases of fire artifacts and stories that survived the smoke and blazes.

Some of these simple remnants of history are little miracles.

A Catholic church tabernacle, taken to the river by a priest, was found intact three days after the fire. A resident's Bible also was found floating in the river.

The remains of a watch helped one family identify the ashes of their home. "In the rush to the river all they took was a blanket which they kept wet and over their heads," wrote a son, W. H. Bentley of Breckenridge, Minnesota. "The blanket saved their lives."

Sidonia Tagatz of Neshkoro donated a brooch and earrings worn by her grandmother on the night of the fire, with this explanation: "Her two sons were running with her to get to the safety of a plowed field when she died of a heart attack. They dropped her and she was found later, burned. They made a casket of charred boards and buried her in the Harmony Cemetery, where other victims of the fire were interred."

Surrounding the fire artifacts are rooms full of typical attire, furnishings, and appliances of the 1870s. These donations came from neighboring towns not damaged by the Peshtigo fire.

The museum is a former Congregational church, and a short stroll outside of it leads to a mass grave where about 350 fire victims who couldn't be identified are buried. About seventy-five of these people

PESHTIGO, THE RIVER

Peshtigo River rafting is a prime reason to visit **Wildman Adventure Resort**, whose two outposts accommodate beginners to experts. Rated Class II to IV rapids, the river's stretches of whitewater are among the Midwest's longest. Excursions are mid-April to mid-October; 45 miles northwest of Peshtigo, the community.

Another option: navigating the wider Menominee River—site of the Midwest's largest rapids—in an eight-person raft. That outpost is 60 miles north, near the Wisconsin-Michigan border.

Ziplining, guided canoeing, hiking, and family-friendly itineraries also are possible. Stay a day or week: riverside campsites and cozy cabins available. wildmanranch.com, (715) 757-2938

lived at the Peshtigo Company's boardinghouse, "so completely consumed by fire that one could not tell man from woman or child from adult." Plaques of explanation also say some bodies were intact, "bearing no trace of burns" but overcome by smoke.

The first Wisconsin State Historical Marker was erected in 1951 at Peshtigo Fire Cemetery to commemorate "the greatest forest fire disaster in American history." Peshtigo Fire Museum is open Memorial Day weekend to October 8, when closing ceremonies include a bell ringing and prayers led by a local pastor. Museum admission is by donation.

Washington Island

Population 777

Sievers School of Fiber Arts

sieversschool.com
(920) 847-2264

To the ecologist, "tension zone" refers to the S-shaped periphery where climate and vegetation shift in Wisconsin. "Up North" begins as oaks diminish, pine forests thicken, and loon calls beckon. Farther north means fewer people and more wildlife.

Being "north of the tension zone" suits Sievers because its rural campus allows for a quieter rhythm of life. Students get to know themselves and others while creating something unique and lasting with their hands.

"You step back in time and do something nice for yourself in a friendly atmosphere," says Ann Young, co-owner with her husband, Howard "Butch" Young. "You set your own goals." Students—beginners, experts, and the in-between—have traveled from all fifty states and eleven foreign countries since the school opened in 1979.

On a wall is a wool quilt of clothing scraps, sewn before the Civil War. Near it is a contemporary quilt by the late Doreen Speckmann, from Wisconsin but internationally known and a former Sievers instructor.

Class work and instruction happen in two roomy, light-filled studios. In a converted barn are beds in a dorm-like setting with shared kitchen and bathrooms. Some students opt for lodging at a condo, resort, or hotel on the island of 35 square miles.

What each student makes depends on the class theme: basketry, beadwork, embroidery, knitting, quilting, dyeing fabrics or paper. Some go home with a new hat, vest, jacket, willow chair, or jewelry ensemble.

Weavers might make a rag rug or learn Navajo techniques. *Temari* stitchery refers to a Japanese folk art. *Shibori* is a Japanese form of tie-dyeing. All are in the Sievers schedule.

FAST FACTS

Four Icelandic settlers landed on Washington Island in 1870, and descendants still call it home. Other immigrants arrived, too, but the island remains one of the nation's oldest Icelandic settlements and among the largest outside of Iceland.

Check out **Rock Island State Park**, the least visited in Wisconsin because two ferry rides are required to get there. In Viking Hall at the Boat House are reminders of Icelandic and Scandinavian heritage. Example: hand-carved oak furniture. dnr.wisconsin.gov, (920) 847-2235

"Rarely do these students do just one thing," Ann says, and classes sometimes overlap. So, a student might knit and weave, try batik and stitch during one island getaway. Also in the class lineup are carving sessions because, as Ann notes, "wood is a fiber, too."

A sister business, Sievers Benchwork, makes wooden table kits for model train hobbyists. "A small town can make things happen," she believes. sieversbenchwork.com, (920) 847-2264

Walter Schutz was 79 when he established Sievers and named the retreat after his wife, Sophie Sievers Schutz, an accomplished hobbyist weaver. Until 2015, when it became harder to obtain parts, Sievers made weaving looms, too.

"Happiness is in your hands and it keeps you young" was the founder's slogan. Three dozen classes, late May through October, are taught by instructors from throughout the country.

Washington Island is a 30-minute boat ride from the top of Door County and 7 miles from the mainland. "When you get on the ferry, the rest of the world stays behind for a while," Ann notes.

Some students stay connected all year and develop a kinship. "She's one of ours," Ann remarks, when the name of a known alum is mentioned. On the Sievers website: "It is telling that so many who discover Sievers return, year after year. Only a place that is loved, that inspires and that transforms can make such a claim."

Not artsy? At Sievers, in an 1890 one-room schoolhouse, is a consignment shop of fiber arts. For sale are the works of eighty-some students and teachers, plus materials for your own fiber art project. Inventory includes fine yarns from Scotland.

FAST FIVE

Farm-to-table dining gets serious attention at **Hotel Washington**, whose owner has encouraged young farmers to relocate and grow ingredients for the hotel restaurant. Serving a gourmet menu of "littles," "middles," and "mains" that skillfully rolls with whatever is in season. Add an overnight: in the 1904 hotel are eight guest rooms. hotelwashingtonandstudio.com, (920) 847-3010

Sunset Resort, open since 1902, makes crepe-like Icelandic pancakes with cherry-rhubarb sauce for breakfast. Or order Swedish *limpa* bread, Norwegian grilled toast (with a crumb coating). Fine sunset views. Closed during winter. sunsetresortwi.com, (920) 847-2531

Open for midweek services during summer is the wooden **Stavekirk** church, crafted by island volunteers in the same manner that sturdy Viking ships were built. Trinity Evangelical Lutheran owns the rugged reminder of Norwegian heritage. trinitylutheran-wi.com/stavkirke, (920) 847-2341

Nelsen's Hall, open since 1899, is the oldest legally and continuously operating saloon in Wisconsin. More bitters (per capita) are drunk there than any place else. During Prohibition, the proprietor got a pharmacist's license so he could dispense a stomach tonic—90 proof bitters— to his customers. Drink a shot of bitters today to get into the Nelsen's Hall Bitters Club. On Facebook, (920) 847-2496

Forget the sand: at the base of **Schoolhouse Beach**, in a protected harbor, are smooth stones. Look and swim, but don't take them. Only four other beaches in the world are like this one. Island signs point the way.

For more about the island and its charms: washingtonisland.com, (920) 847-2179.

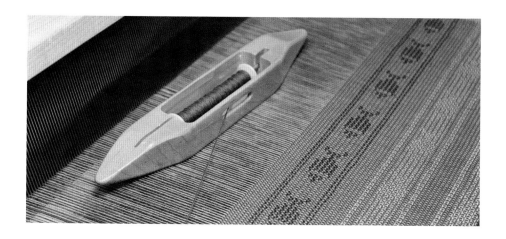

Cultural Coalition of Wisconsin (for events, resources about arts, culture, history, humanities): portalwisconsin.org, (608) 266-0190.

Dairy Farmers of Wisconsin (for cheese, cheesemaker, cheese factory info): wisconsincheese.com, (608) 836-8820.

Destinations Wisconsin (for convention and visitors bureaus: destinationswisconsin.com, (608) 837-6693.

Ice Age Trail Alliance (for Ice Age National Scenic Trail maps, hiking advice, volunteer work opportunities along the 1,000-mile footpath): iceagetrail.org, (800) 227-0046.

Wisconsin Agricultural Tourism Association (for farm-based destinations): wiagtourism.com, (608) 774-1354.

Wisconsin Bed and Breakfast Association (for lodging in owner-occupied premises that include breakfast): wbba.org, (715) 942-8180.

Wisconsin Brewers Guild (for brewery locations): wibrewersguild.com, (608) 567-3690.

Wisconsin Department of Natural Resources (for info about state parks, trails, other natural recreational outlets, and relevant regulations): dnr.wisconsin.gov, (888) 936-7463.

Wisconsin Department of Tourism (for destination descriptions, event listings, regional updates on fall colors and snow conditions for winter sports): travelwisconsin.com, (800) 432-8747.

Wisconsin Department of Transportation (for road conditions): 511wi.gov, wisconsindot.gov, (866) 511-9472.

Wisconsin Distillers Guild (for distillery locations): wisconsindistillersguild.org.

Wisconsin Historical Society (for the state's official historical sites, markers, and museums): wisconsinhistory.org, (608) 261-9583.

Wisconsin Rustic Roads (for maps and descriptions of scenic backroads throughout the state; download or order the guide): wisconsindot.gov.

Wisconsin Winery Association (for winery locations): wisconsinwineries.org, (920) 478-4499.

Acknowledgments

No book of substance is created single-handedly.

My deep appreciation goes to municipal officials and public librarians in so many of Wisconsin's small towns. The work you do is important, and that includes helping to answer all kinds of annoying questions during my book research.

Reps for chambers of commerce, visitor bureaus, and destinations were extremely helpful, too, especially Julia Hertel of Destinations Wisconsin, Jon Jarosh and Jen Rogers of Destination Door County, and Ken Leiviska of Boelter + Lincoln.

Thank you, photographers for Castlerock Museum (page 9), Green County Tourism (cover, page 22), Dorf Haus (page 34), Taliesin Preservation (page 35), American Players Theatre (page 37), Wisconsin Historical Society (page 52), Luxembourg American Cultural Society Inc. (pages 58, 61), Midwest Renewable Energy Association (page 64), Farm Aid (page 67), Road America (page 69), Elkhart Lake Chamber of Commerce (page 71), Ten Chimneys (page 74), Kohler Company (pages 83, 87), Trek Bicycle Corporation (pages 98, 99), Yerkes Observatory (pages 101, 102), Wisconsin Great Northern Railroad (cover, pages 106, 133), Bayfield Chamber and Visitor Bureau (pages 108, 121), American Birkebeiner Ski Foundation (page 112), Canoe Bay Escape Village (page 115), Sawmill Pizza and Brew Shed (page 119), Lumberjack World Championships (page 125), Boulder Junction Chamber of Commerce (pages 140, 149), von Stiehl Winery (page 143), Eagle River Area Chamber of Commerce (page 153), Iola Old Car Show (page 169), and Min-Aqua Bats (page 176). Your good work complements my own photography.

I am grateful for the keen eyes of my former co-workers: copy editors Lynn Danielson, Judie Kleinmaier, Steve Lund and Mark Lundey, plus my razor-sharp partner for life, Richard Franken. All helped me give a final edit to what you see here.

The work of staff at Rowman & Littlefield/Globe Pequot is valued highly too, particularly that of Amy Lyons, former editorial director; Jehanne Schweitzer, senior production editor; and Cooper Filhaber, assistant acquisitions editor.

Index

About the Author

Small-Town Wisconsin is Mary Bergin's sixth book and one that feels dear because she has long paid attention to the unique, exceptional, and quirky in rural America. Her writing forte is travel, food, heritage, and sustainability—especially in the Midwest and particularly in her home state of Wisconsin.

Content for this new book is a mix of new material and previously published works that she updated. The lifelong journalist spent decades working in newsrooms as an editor or reporter for Wisconsin, Indiana, Kentucky, and Oklahoma newspapers. She switched to full-time free-lance work in 2008 and is a four-time winner of a Lowell Thomas Award, the highest national recognition for travel journalists.

Her work has been published widely through online and print media outlets, including Tribune Content Agency and the USA Today Network. *Wisconsin Supper Club Cookbook* was her fifth book. She is a member of the Society of American Travel Writers, North American Travel Journalists Association, and Midwest Travel Journalists Association.

The Wisconsin native grew up on a small dairy farm in Sheboygan County and has lived in Madison since 1988, sharing a home with her longtime partner, Richard, and their two adorable cats, Siena and Doolin.

Follow her at marybergin.com, roadstraveled.com, or smalltownhues.com.